Uncle Harve and Miss Lucille

A Legacy

Bessie Mayes

BookLocker

Saint Petersburg, Florida

Paperback ISBN: 978-1-64718-474-2
Hardcover ISBN: 978-1-64718-475-9
Epub ISBN: 978-1-64718-476-6
Mobi ISBN: 978-1-64718-477-3

Published by BookLocker.com, Inc., St. Petersburg, Florida.

Printed on acid-free paper.

BookLocker.com, Inc.
2020

First Edition

Library of Congress Cataloging in Publication Data
Mayes, Bessie
Uncle Harve and Miss Lucille: A Legacy by Bessie Mayes
Library of Congress Control Number: 2020914137

Dedication

This book is dedicated to my parents' legacy, my siblings and their families. In particular, our Sister Mom Bettye. She has been the point of wisdom for me and my siblings. She read parts of this book that I had completed, and gave me advice. She encouraged me very often to work on the book daily, and seemed to know when I had dropped off production. So, she checked more than a few times to see how far I had progressed. However, and most important, this book is dedicated to Yeshua ha Mashiach. Jesus the Messiah. He really wrote the book. Our book. I did this for His and the Kingdom's Glory, as He reminded me of His word daily. The book follows the life of a couple who left a legacy of hope, trust, and love for their children, and those generations that followed in their footsteps. This book explores that in depth, and how that couple achieved much success leaving that legacy with their children, their grandchildren, and their great-great grandchildren. This book includes elements of slavery that forged a strength of character, perseverance, and fortitude within the family then, and the family now.

We still continue to live for Jesus and helping others to come to know him in our everyday encounters with people and their life. Hopefully this book will inspire you and your family too. Dor l' Dor. From generations to generations.

Daddy and Mama had one scripture that was the standard of our house, and that they repeated if necessary, to whomever was there living a long time or short. It was Joshua 24:14:

"And if it seems evil to you to serve the Lord, choose for yourselves this day whom you will serve, whether the gods which your fathers served that *were* on the other side of the River, or the gods of the Amorites, in whose land you dwell. But as for me and my house, we will serve the Lord."

Table of Contents

Introduction 1

Chapter 1: Uncle Harve and Miss Lucille: a legacy of faith, compassion, hope, and love.. 3

Chapter 2: In the beginning: courtship 7

Chapter 3: Daddy's employer: the Hinshaws.. 9

Chapter 4: As we grew older: Macedonia Church 17

Chapter 5: But our house caught on fire 21

Chapter 6: Only ones in a beautiful place 27

Chapter 7: After Dr. Martin Luther King and President John Kennedy; Taylorsville High School 33

Chapter 8: Fertile grounds 39

Chapter 9: Come the holidays: Thanksgiving and Christmas. "For Me and my house, we will serve the Lord." 43

Chapter 10: The more, the merrier, at times... 49

Chapter 11: Love of Sundays... 59

Chapter 12: Macedonia, meals, and we loved Sundays 63

Chapter 13: Aunt/Miss Lucile and Mama Judy: their legacy.................... 71

Chapter 14: Mama, the Lord shows His seers in advance 97

Chapter 15: Daddy's lineage and Macedonia Baptist Church............... 105

Chapter 16: All about Bettye and Russell; and the Lackeys 111

Chapter 17: Jessie (Buster) Mayes 129

Chapter 18: Howard (Pee-Wee) Mayes 135

Chapter 19: James Mayes 149

Chapter 20: Mary Mayes: My constant roommate 161

Chapter 21: Harvey Mayes Junior 167

Chapter 22: Bessie Mayes; Out of the ashes of Hell to triumph 175

Introduction

Genesis 1:1 In the beginning, God created the heavens and the earth.

Genesis 1:26-27: And God said, "Let Us make man in Our image, after Our likeness; and let them have dominion over the fish of the sea, and over the fowl of the air, and over the cattle, and over all the earth and over every creeping thing that creepeth upon the earth." So, God created man in His own image, in the image of God created He him; male and female created He them."

We are all descendants of the living God. Made in His image and His likeness. The Son of God, Jesus, from this scripture, also created the family that He would later be born into. A family that brought Him both joy and sadness when a few of His siblings, not His mother Mary and brothers James and Jude, may have deserted him at his most painful and crucial time as He prepared to die as the Messiah on the cross. Imagine, Jesus the Son of God and our Savior, created the family that he would be born into. He could have easily developed a home where his opinions would always be respected and shared throughout His vast family. I would have. But He knew that the family he would be born into would not entirely be in support of Him or his mission on earth in the end. Free will. Yet, also thanks to Jesus the Son of God, He showed His creation how to deal with family, relatives, and friends in the larger scheme of eternity.

Jesus was born into a family that would, in the end, explore relationship issues while He was on earth.

Matthew 12:47-50: So, someone said to him: "Look! Your mother and your brothers are standing outside, seeking to speak to you." In reply he said to the one who spoke to him: "Who is my mother, and who are my brothers?" And extending his hand toward his disciples, he said: "Look! My mother and my brothers! For whoever does the will of my Father who is in heaven, that one is my brother and sister and mother."

The Lord placed on my heart to write this book about our family. But earlier, in 2015, I began to write a book just about myself and the ministry that God had developed for me in various churches and synagogues. In 2018, God changed the focus of that book into the one you are reading here: the loving, kind, and wonderful legacy of Harve and Lucille Mayes, my parents. Having noted the verses above and just as Jesus did even siblings carried on their Mayes legacy. In fact, Jesus's family was a template for Christian families, because issues do arise in them. And it took a Savior/Redeemer who has been here and done that to show us the way to resolve them. In the end, God gets the Glory, as Jesus did when He returned to Heaven in victory for all generations then and all generations that follow in His Word.

Chapter 1:
Uncle Harve and Miss Lucille: a legacy of faith, compassion, hope, and love

The beginning of a family—the farm, and the Hinshaws

My childhood is what formed mine and our family's foundation for a good life.

Our family grew up in Taylorsville, North Carolina. We lived in a quiet middle-class/upper middle-class community in a rural area, a few miles out of town. Our home was a two-story house sitting on a large plot of land.

Our house had a very large plot, with a yard front, sides, and back. Part of the backyard was also the area where Daddy placed gravel rocks for a parking vehicle, with a wraparound driveway. The way our father engineered things, the gravel also allowed for easy movement for us and other people should it rain.

Near that area was a building built with cinderblocks called the "Well House." Back in the earlier days of their lives, this was used by my parents to "draw" a bucket of water. The house didn't have running water in the earlier beginning of their marriage. I mention this building because, as a child, my curiosity got the best of me. Afraid of spiders and snakes, both of whom were constant occupiers, I pretty much avoided it.

In my early childhood years, my parents gave me a tour:

Mama and Daddy allowed me to see the water after removing items stacked over the opening of the entrance to the well that kept inquisitive little children like me out. It was very deep, very dark, and very scary. Daddy said the water was cold and tasted sweet. As I became older, I was reminded of this well when I was sent to my cousin's house to play. While there with my cousin Mildred (Mill), daughter-in-law to my Dad's sister, I had to draw water using a pump. Their house didn't have indoor plumping during the period I was there, but they did get it later. That was interesting to do, and hard for a little girl as I was. I'm certain Mama and Daddy didn't miss drawing water when they got indoor plumbing. But the well was the early days of our parents' existence. Our lifestyle improved greatly as our family grew.

Our home, with its large size, also had large covering trees in the front and backyards; trees that shielded us from the sun and shaded us. The trees' canopies were also a place where people parked cars in the many of my memories where the yard was full of cars, due to my brother's barbershop business and visits from family and friends. As the yard filled with visitors during the course of an afternoon, we moved with the sun as it rotated. Mama would say to the crowd there for a visit, "Well, it's time to move over here out of the sun." We'd all pick up our lawn chairs at that point and moved to where she wanted us to sit. Needless to say, there were jokes. "Okay, I get to sit closer to the shade this time," while we looked up to the sun for the best angle away from the beams. And for those sitting on their cars chatting with others, the complaint was "I've gotta move this car 'cause it's gettin' too hot on this hood."

I remember as an adult having to mow all the sections of this large yard with a push mower. Even though we owned a riding lawn mower, I never used it as I believed that it couldn't cut as neatly as the push mower underneath the long hedges and trees that bordered the yards on each side. However, I have to give credit to my brothers, who did use a riding lawn mower successfully after I moved away. Perhaps I could have saved myself from being sunburned had I employed their techniques! They, by the way, tried to tell me that all the time I lived there and maintained the place. The boys—Pee-Wee, Jim, and nephew Jamie—were the ones who took over those duties for Mama and Daddy when I did leave. And they did a much better job!

The home had large rooms. My six siblings and I took up most of the rooms. The boys slept upstairs, and Mary and I slept downstairs. But our parents used the bedroom on the front of the house to remain as a guest room after our oldest sister Bettye moved off to Livingston College in Salisbury, North Carolina. But this land was not owned by us, nor the house that we lived in. All of it belonged to Daddy's employer, Mr. Luther M. Hinshaw, since it was located on his estate property. But Mr. Hinshaw and his wife never really perceived this as such, and called it Mama and Daddy's place, as did others in town. So, how did our parents get there? This is how the story and legacy begins about "Uncle Harve" and "Miss Lucille."

Chapter 2:
In the beginning: courtship

My mom and dad met and dated where she lived on Todd's Mountain. She and her numerous siblings owned land there too. Daddy had a car, and apparently was pretty popular. Or perhaps he was pretty witty. But we were told that when he saw Mama, he broke up with the woman he was dating. In fact, the woman he broke up with was, ironically, the mother of a boyfriend I would date decades later in high school. My Mom often teased me about that, as did his Mother. "So-and-so could have been your mother instead of me," Mama would tease. I believe that a long while after marriage, Daddy decided that instead of farming the land of his ancestors as he initially had planned to do, he'd get a job to support her and provide shelter or a home for her and any children in the future. Thus, his employment with Roger Hinshaw.

Chapter 3:
Daddy's employer: the Hinshaws

Carolyn Hinshaw, heir to the estate, came across the road to talk with
Mama (sitting). My brother Jr. and Mary look on.

Carolyn and Mama

Mr. Luther M. Hinshaw owned stores in other towns and counties. The large main store in the town of Taylorsville served as his headquarters. Nicknamed the Dime Store, it had a variety of household products, candies, sewing necessities with cloth by the yard, and a large supply of various crafting-related products. The store actually was a general store with lots of interesting products that people needed for men, women, and children, but at a reasonable price for sale. Many people came in because of the friendly staff, but also because it offered what they needed for their households and school products. Their office was on the second floor, overlooking much of the main part of the store. Mr. Hinshaw would arrive after he had finished eating his breakfast with his wife and family, which was cooked by a maid. Other maids serviced their house daily with other duties, which included cleaning, the laundry, and keeping up the landscape. He had one daughter, Carolyn S.

Hinshaw. Her mother was Sarah Hinshaw. Various other people lived there with them. Janie Hare shared the Hinshaw household, although she was not known as being related by birth to anyone in the family.

Every morning at eight o'clock, except Sundays, my father would go "across the road," a colloquial term meant to indicate that one of us was at the Hinshaw's house. Usually Daddy drove Mr. Hinshaw to work at his store. Highway 90 was a busy thoroughfare most of the day, with a heavy traffic jam in the afternoon from multiple furniture plants' employees going home. The two-lane road separated our houses, Hinshaw's and Mama and Daddy's, directly in front of our houses. I noted growing up there as a child how Mr. Hinshaw, with Daddy driving, left at the same time as other business owners or managers in our neighborhood to go to work at his store...well, after the traffic jam of most people at 5 to 6 a.m., until when they left around 8. This is not to disrespect our neighborhood. In fact, five of us ended up taking the same route as adults, including Mama. She worked at Broyhill Furniture for over twenty years before retiring. That's when she said to me that, as she lay in bed, she could hear that early-morning traffic heading to work. And all she had to do was laugh, roll over, and go back to sleep. Well deserved, I believe!

Mr. Hinshaw also owned homes along the route to town. He rented them out to people as he did us. But we never paid rent or utilities because that was a perk he gave to Daddy and Mama. He did pay Daddy a salary in addition to that perk. When my oldest sibling Bettye enrolled in college, Mr. Hinshaw paid for her first year. Bettye later became a highly acclaimed teacher and a leader in her town, county, and the nation. She achieved two master's degrees, all related to the educational field she loved.

The Mayes and Hinshaw families intermingled on many occasions, as we did with the other families in our community. Lots of "crossing the road" to go from one house to another. There were visitations, swimming in their pool, playing as children on the land across the road and behind our house.

Daddy had planted gardens beside our house and behind theirs. Also, Mrs. Hinshaw had rabbits. Mary really loved going to see them. I barely remember them, but I do remember that they were in a pen in back of their house. And they were white and fluffy. I'm glad I learned quite a few years later that the Hinshaws kept the population down by giving away or perhaps eating them. I don't really know.

Behind our house was a large barn that was used for storing hay and horses that belonged to Carolyn, the owner's daughter. She rode horses in shows to earn ribbons and trophies. She was very accomplished and had been trained by a professional on how to compete. She won a lot of first-class trophies, or was not far behind in being in the top ten. I remember as a child going to one with my father, who drove the horse trailer. He finally relented and allowed me to go. I saw Carolyn wearing a rider's gear, which included a tall black hat, riding pants with her pants leg tucked into her black riding boots, and a fancy white blouse. I had never seen her in any competition before that. That was when I fell in love with horses and horse shows. I still follow the equestrian competitions when I can, and watch the Triple Crown series every year. And as I grew a little older, she let me dust a bit in some areas of the Hinshaw house on Saturday mornings. I got to make five dollars for a couple of hours polishing those trophies. When I did, I would ask Daddy to take me to Carolyn's Dime Store, where I would purchase makeup and other items that would interest an eleven-year-old girl.

One day, Carolyn asked me a question. She said, "You know, Bess, I pay you money for the two-hour job, and then you come to my store and buy stuff. Don't you think that you are just handing me back the money for work I paid you for?" Made sense, I thought, a little embarrassed. So, I began to save the money for trips when Mama and Daddy were going for groceries.

The Hinshaw Estate Seat (house)

Also, as another perk, Mr. Luther Hinshaw allowed Daddy and any guests he wanted to accompany him to fish in the three private large ponds that were in the forest behind their main house. The upper pond was for swimming, and was where we as children spent a lot of summers. And the one pond down from it had been filled with bluegill fish. When Daddy wanted to just fish for himself, he would ask me to go find some worms. Those worms were located at this barn. I took the pitchfork and dug into the ground at the front door. That was where the horse manure was. This was the spot where Carolyn, the county winner, would mount or dismount her horses. So, while they stood there to either be saddled or unsaddled normally by her and friends, they pooped. Daddy had taught me as a little girl how to dig for the worms. I thought the worms were bad enough. But having to dig them out of manure was disgusting. But I got used to it. Daddy didn't send me all the time, just when he wouldn't have the time to spend on that part of the operation prior to catching fish. I placed the pitchfork into an area as he had told me to do and firmly pulled back on the handle. Then, as Daddy showed me, I turned the manure over into the tin cup container he used to hold the worms. I hated seeing them wiggle around, so I usually made a quick beeline for the house, worms in tow.

This barn was the site of many activities. For example, a really authentic boxing ring was built by Daddy upstairs in the loft for Buster, who revered Floyd Patterson, a professional boxer. The boxing ring was impressive, with three real large ropes placed in a square, creating the ring.

Buster (Jessie) asked his brothers and friends, and grabbed some other family members, to box in a real match. He acted as the referee, of course. Plus, Daddy was there watching to ensure that the boxers and the boxing didn't get out of hand. I was barred from being there after my first time, because Daddy wanted just the teens and older boys to participate in the audience and the boxing. But since this was the place where the Hinshaws put their hay, and because of possible liabilities to the estate if someone was injured, we had to stop the fun.

The barn has fallen down now.

But the boys and Buster's friends outside the community got an experience that was otherwise only seen on television. "Uncle Harve" had given the families of the boys a summer that would never be forgotten. Such fun! Sometime later, Mr. Hinshaw allowed Daddy to build a dirt race track in the middle of a wooded area behind the barn, so we could race our go-carts without disturbing our neighbors. This track was elaborate, with twists and turns. And a straightaway to the finish line. As I said before, the track was carved out deep inside the woods that belonged to the Hinshaws. And no one in or around our neighborhood was bothered anymore by the noise. Decades later, Carolyn built a very large barn directly beside their home. It held twenty horse stalls, sleeping quarters for the barn staff, a private room for the trainer, and an office/open living area for events. Thus, the wooden barn ceased to be used.

Chapter 4:
As we grew older: Macedonia Church

There are seven of us that lived

Mama had four children who passed away unexpectedly at various times and ages. I learned this one day from my father. And so, I asked Mama about what had happened to them. The first one born had a heart defect and died from it. She was a little girl whose name was Jeanette. The next time Mama got pregnant she birthed a son whose name was Adam. He died from crib death syndrome. I'm unsure how the third baby passed, but it could have had something to do with the delivery procedure with the midwife. The next baby lived to be much older than the first two, but passed away too. Her name was Jo Ann, and she was nicknamed "Hoppy." She was something special to Mama and Daddy. Mama told me that they had given her the nickname because she brought so much joy to their home with her antics and smile. She was an active eleven-month-old child who brought light to their marriage again after the premature deaths of the little babies. But she too succumbed to ill health and died.

The next time our sibling, Bettye, made it, although with a heart condition. The rest of us came later, three years apart. After Bettye came Jessie, Howard, James, Mary, myself, and Harvey Jr. That was by instruction from the hospital doctor, to have our children at least two to three years apart. And Mama and Daddy did just that. One of the main reasons was because Mama had almost lost James (Jim) to a breech. The story was told to me by my brother Buster and Mary. He said he and Pee-Wee were very, very young. They were told by Daddy to go outside and play one day. So, they did. While outside, they noticed that the family doctor was walking up the backyard sidewalk into the house. Buster said he was carrying a black "bag" or case. Buster said that this caught our attention. So, he and Pee-Wee decided to go into the house to see why he had come. Before they could get into the back-porch door, Daddy came out and told them sternly, "Go play!" So, they left and stood outside there in the backyard. Soon after the doctor went into the house, he came out. Buster said, "that's when we heard this noise." So, they again attempted go near the house. He said the noise sounded like something he nor others had heard before. So, they snuck back inside the house. He said they saw Mama and Daddy in the bedroom and saw a baby wrapped in a blanket. Buster said that then he and Pee-Wee knew why they'd heard that "noise."

Later, Buster said that he had noticed that "Mama was fat. But then she wasn't fat anymore." He said that he and Pee-Wee had wondered what the doctor had in his bag. Then he and Pee-Wee decided that the doctor had brought the baby in that bag, and had given the baby to Mama and Daddy. He said, "I asked Daddy why Mama had lost all that weight." Daddy still refused to answer. Buster said that none of them knew where babies came from during that time in their lives. But a starker part to this story, told by my sister Mary, was the reason the doctor had to come. She said that the midwife had come outside the bedroom "wringing her hands." Daddy, who was working in the fields, was called to come home, because the birth had hit a crisis. So, when Daddy got there, he called or told whoever called him to call their primary doctor. Soon after, that was when Buster and Pee-Wee saw him arrive outside while they were listening at the windows and doors. He came in and turned Jim around in Mama's womb. He then birthed the child.

That is when Buster said that the "rest of you"—meaning Mary, myself, and Junior—were birthed in a hospital. Daddy and Mama never used a midwife again. I said that up until Jim. They used one who was used by many in that day and time due to lack of access to hospitals or expense in delivering babies in the hospitals. Even Mary had to be taken to another hospital in another city to be birthed without any hesitation. No way was Mama and Daddy ever going to use a midwife again to birth their children. However, Buster and Pee-Wee still believed, until they got older, that Jim arrived there in that doctor's "bag."

We loved going to church. In the summer, our Mama and Daddy would dress in their finest suits. We children would be dressed in our finest clothes. I remember my sister Mary and I wearing identical dresses, bows in our hair, and little socks with lace around the turned-down edge of the sock. I was dressed in a blue dress as Mary wore a pink one. We were not twins, but we were about the same height and body frame. Mary was always referred to as being tiny or little though. That was just her body structure at that age. Now she did stay that way as an adult too, remaining tiny. Junior, being the youngest, wore a shirt, a dress coat, and a bow tie. He looked very cute as a child. Not too bad looking now either.

The older boys, of course, had on nice suits and shoes. Buster even had a pair of white loafers. They were just like Elvis Presley's supposed "blue suede shoes." Buster's were white, and didn't need a lot of attention. He would polish and buff his black shoes on Saturdays to wear on Sundays. But the white suedes were his pride and joy. Mama loved that he had them, and smiled when teased by his friends and brothers about them. She was just happy for him, because it made him happy.

Mama and Daddy always rejoiced with us, and they were sad for us when life was not going so well. They both were always happy for us and loved us. We wanted to garner their approval, because we loved them some much too. They meant the world to us. We loved and adored them back and wanted to always be good and have their favor. No pressure, because it was based biblically. In Psalm 21, King David prays to God. "He lets me rest in green pasture, leads me beside calm waters. He restores my soul and leads me in the path of righteousness for HIS NAMESAKE."

Even though some of us were not fully believers then, the one thing all of us had in common was that we wanted to follow in the path of righteousness for "our parents' sake." They set the Godly example, and we wanted to follow the example they set as Christian parents as close as possible. Yes, our Pastor Rev. Moore preached on God's way and God's love for His flock there. And we heard him every week, which helped keep those wonderful morals at least. Peer pressure from those other relatives in our family like Aunt Did (Margaret), Mrs. Lucille (Uncle Plez's sister), Uncle Plez, Aunt Mag (Margaret), Aunt East (both Daddy's sisters), Aunt Blanch and her daughter Aunt Sarah, and Uncle Wade (husband to Sarah) also helped us grow more in God's path. We siblings did so willingly with respect for their input. So, Mama was so happy that Buster was happy for the nice white suede shoes and a white dress jacket.

Chapter 5:
But our house caught on fire

God is compassionate.

It was a big house. One day, Daddy and Mama had discussed how we all would get out of the house if it caught on fire. Then, they both got us together to practice the drill. It was during a weekend. They sent us to our regular spots in the house. The boys slept upstairs, so Daddy sent them there. We girls were downstairs, so they sent us to our room. Daddy went to the boys' room and had them practice getting out the upstairs windows to the front roof, which was just off their bedrooms. The girls watched outside in the front yard. We saw how Daddy had them climb out of the bedroom window and then how to get off the roof safely. Then he took us girls and showed us how to exit the window upstairs to the roof, and if downstairs, out the kitchen door, which was on the back of the house. We all had a lot of fun with this, especially the boys, who loved the fact that they could climb out on the front roof and drop carefully to the porch and escape. Once we were all back together, Daddy and Mama gave explicit instructions on where we all would gather so they could get a head count. I was assigned a spot in the large hay field near an old tire. We all went back into the house. But from then on, on hot nights the boys would sneak out onto the roof off their bedrooms and sleep. Well, until Mama found out and yelled at them to stop doing it. Daddy just laughed.

I was coming home on our school bus. It was around three-thirty in the afternoon. I saw a horrible scene. There were fire trucks in our side driveway. The driveway circled the house like a horseshoe. I saw smoke coming out of the front of the house upstairs. I saw cars parked on the side of the highway, some looking at the fire. Sad looks. I was told by one of my siblings to go to where Daddy had told me to go. And I did, right to the tire in the hay field. But the other siblings were supposed to join up with me, as Daddy had said for the final count. No one was there but me. I was alone, watching my house on fire. I waited there a long time in disbelief. My house was burning down in front of me.

I wanted to find where my family was because at that point all I saw were firemen and strangers running to and fro. I got my courage up to act, and I decided to find them. I walked into the front yard, looking for any of my brothers. I found later that Pee-Wee and Jim had been upstairs with Mama too. They were throwing our cloths out the back and front windows upstairs over the kitchen. That area was where the fire had started. I never saw Mary or Junior during this time, which left me even more afraid. After entering through the open door of the hedge I saw Buster. Then I saw Mama carrying out clothing, including Buster's white coat, and laying them across the other hedge on the other side of the driveway. She looked horrible. I have never seen my Mama so upset, to this day still. She went back into the front door of the house. I walked around to the back of the house and saw smoke billowing out the back upstairs window. I was in shock, as I know it now today. I walked out to what we called the first driveway. That is when I saw the firemen and neighbors carrying Mama out and across the street to our neighbor's house—actually Daddy's employer, Hinshaw. Mama was weeping and crying hysterically.

I had seen earlier that Mama had found Buster's suede shoes and had laid them on the hedge too, white against the green color of the hedge. By this time, traffic had slowed to a crawl. A few cars were there because of the fire, but others looked with shock and hurt as the house burned. Our parents were referred to by the townsfolks as either "Mr. Harve" and "Miss Lucille" or "Uncle Harve" and "Aunt Lucille." This day, all they knew was that the people they knew and loved had their house on fire.

It was easy crossing for the firemen carrying Mama over to the Hinshaws' house. I followed them, hearing my Mother wailing in hysteria. Two men had her legs, another two had her arms on her upper body. But she didn't care. All she wanted was to go back into the house and get our stuff out. I stayed with Mama. But as I turned to look back at our house, I saw black smoke curling out of the second-story windows. I went into shock. I was told by an adult to go inside "the house." The Hinshaw house. That's where I finally saw Mary and Junior. They had been taken over there earlier by a few firemen.

After everything, all the turmoil, all the water trucks, and all the cars and people had gone and things had subsided, it was dark outside. The house fire was put out. Some of the house didn't catch, though. The back part of the house where the kitchen was, and the upstairs where the boys slept, was burned. Much of the front part of the house had been saved. I don't remember a lot about what happened afterwards. But I do remember that in the front part of the house, our living room, was where we stayed that night. I will never forget the smell of the house while it was burning, and afterwards when we sat there in the front room. My little brother and I were the youngest. Daddy told us that people had offered to take us in, and the other siblings too until the house was rebuilt. But in that front room, sitting with them, we children banded together.

The older siblings had been offered places with their friends since their rooms upstairs had been partially burned, so they had to go. But they had said no too at first. When Daddy told me and Junior that they had found a place for us, we said no, that we were staying in the house. So, Junior and I stayed with Mama and Daddy. They made us stay in the living room for fear of some kind of danger in the rest of the house. And perhaps too, the lasting impression of the damage done to it by the fire. For me, that was well-thought concern. I still remember the fire to this very day. Imagine seeing half your house charred and gutted with only burned-out logs left behind. One of my other siblings had been burned by the fire. Buster, my oldest brother, had decided to give his suede shoes away to a friend. He said that Mama could have died in the fire going back for them. This haunted him for a while, but with Mama's help, he got over it.

After a few months passed, we all had moved back into the house. We had learned that each sibling was important, and how much we loved each other and our parents. Did we stop the infighting among ourselves? I really think so. We called a truce in that we never let our tempers get too heated, even though our parents had tried to get us to do that as we grew older for years.

Chapter 6:
Only ones in a beautiful place

Our neighbors were people who owned businesses like the town newspaper, or were white-collar workers for other businesses in and among other areas or surrounding cities. My brothers and sisters and I sometimes played with the children of these families. We grew up knowing no differences in status or race, as the community was loving and kind. But the signs from the past that said "Colored People" in other parts of town were how some people once entered a few of the businesses a while back. Didn't harm Daddy or Mama, as they always entered through the front doors without hesitation nor incident. The Caucasians all over treated him and Mama and our family like everyone else.

I do remember a business that I had been told in my childhood days was once segregated. The building was a few doors down from the Dime Store where Daddy worked, and its name was "Smithy's." The store sold clothing primarily for men, but included women's clothes too. Household goods or items were on the basement floor. The store's clothing was very expensive, so I never lingered there after a short visit. But the store also offered a cafeteria in their basement that served the people who worked in town, because there weren't many restaurants in the town at that time. I had been sent there many times to get food for Daddy if he wanted to keep working on putting together his inventory for Hinshaw's stores in other counties. He told me where to go for entry. I did so. I entered and saw Flonie, her nickname, a close friend to our family. She greeted me and asked what I wanted to eat. I got the food and left.

A long time later, as I was attending Wilkes Community College, I was given a job by the manager, Helen Robinson. I had to earn money for my tuition that fall for college. One day the manager, who also was good friends with my parents and lived nearby, asked me to accompany her to Smithy's for lunch. Our families were very close; she and her husband Harold had once spent Halloween together in our house as we waited for the trick-or-treaters. Here and again, this was the normal way our community was. Back at town, and as Helen and I walked down the street, I noticed that we entered Smithy's through the front door of the store. As we did, she shouted hellos to the staff and customers whom she knew. They smiled at me too, as I walked with her. I wonder where Helen, who was leading me, was going. At the back of the store there were stairs that went down. As we descended, we entered the cafeteria, the same one where I was told to enter at the back by my father. Helen yelled hellos to everyone as we went to sit down at the cafeteria's chairs.

I realized that I had never seen this part of the store. There was a wall to the left of us in the cafeteria. When the waitress came to take or orders, Helen asked for her usual. As I looked at other people eating there at the bar, it occurred to me why I was told by Daddy to go to the basement to pick up food. The tradition had been that the store served black people on one side of that wall, and whites at the other side where I was currently sitting. I saw the surprise look on Flonie's face too as she came to service other customers. She looked shocked to see me sitting there. And quite frankly, so was I. But nobody said a word of disrespect to me. Customers at the bar smiled at me too and went back to eating. After lunch, I decided that if I ate there again that I would go to the "white" side because I could. Little did I know what really wasn't the case.

Later on, I learned that the cafeteria was, at one time, segregated. But not at that time I was there. The blacks went to the left side only because it had room, and not because of segregation from whites, and some of them did jobs that made their clothes dirty. These customers, some, didn't really want anyone seeing it. So, they took their plates of food to eat somewhere else other than there. The store, Smithy's, was not segregated as I thought. Old memories in the town existed of that, but the store was no longer operating under that format. And hadn't for decades. We all, customers or anyone, could sit wherever we wanted.

One time, I did ask a black patron about his opinion of sitting on the left side instead of the right side of the cafeteria. His response confirmed what had been said to me before. He wasn't afraid, or abiding, or aware of rules of segregation that had been there in the past. He said, "All the seats were usually taken on the right side." And as for Daddy telling me to enter a different way, that entrance was quicker because it led directly to the second floor where the cafeteria was located. In fact, Daddy knew the owner, Mr. Smithy, and they were friends. Perceptions I held were wrong, as I found out that day. And after seeing the greeting that Mrs. Barnette and I got, that perception was dismissed by me forever. I put it here to show how "erroneous information" can play a part in causing confusion and division. Be aware in your own mind and hearts as well.

"Up town" (Taylorsville); Happy Plains High school

Having grown up as the only black family in our neighborhood was interesting. Our family had no issues with neighbors who were white. We didn't see color. Nor apparently did they. We didn't even know of issues to be had at that time in our lives as youngsters. In fact, Daddy and Mama held the respect for the families living there and in other communities and cities as well. The schools were segregated at that time, however. The irony for my family was this: when we went to school as youngsters in days gone by, we would board a school bus that took us to an all-black school. But when we were returning to our house, we returned to an all-white neighborhood.

Later, as I grew up to the third and fourth grades, I still rode the bus. I noted that buses carrying black students had to go along the back street while the buses carrying white students were allowed to go down the front streets. The school board felt that black kids made too much noise, which was crazy since all children make loud noises on a bus. Then our principal told us that it was because of traffic congestion; the city didn't want too many buses on the front street. Since we got out later in the day, that didn't make sense either. I wondered who these "city officials" were, as I was not used to such treatment due to skin color. *How did they get there?* I often wondered to myself. *I've never met anyone like that,* I thought. Are they just mean?

So, on a few occasions our bus driver, a student, Michael, would not turn to go down the back streets, but would go down the front streets. We were very quiet on the bus. No one spoke. After the ride down a front street, we would break out in loud cheers, which encouraged our bus driver, and that also said, "Please stop this practice!" Michael was a straight-A student. He told me that he would rise every day at 3 a.m. to begin picking up students in the rural areas of the township. Those students on the bus had to also rise early, around six in the morning, to catch the bus, as it was their only way to class. It would be dark when they got on the bus, and daylight when the bus reached our house.

Our family—Mary, Junior, and I—were the last pickups on his route. The bus arrived at our house at eight o'clock. The all black school that we attended at that time started at 8:30 a.m., and let out at 3:30 p.m. Again, that would stagger, we were told, the times buses were on the road. All I can say is that the town was officially desegregated while I was in my junior year in 1967. Our school, Happy Plains High School, was closed too.

The building is now an office complex for various social services for the public. The school board also closed some schools with the idea and hope that as the result, all students would have that experience of attending a new school in their own districts. Not just the black students. That was made clear to us as students as well. Interesting enough, I had hoped to go to a school district that didn't require such a long drive to get there. After I learned how much was at stake for my bus mates to rise just to get to school, I shut up. However, I found out later that in fact, the line was drawn such that our house was the beginning of a new school district east of us in the next town of Hiddenite. The Mayes were not kept in the town district that stretched to our town of Taylorsville. But that really didn't matter to me at this point, as Mama and Daddy purchased a Chevy II for me to drive to my classes at the new school.

Although Daddy worked in town, he couldn't always get to me after school for pickup. Once, before I had the car, I walked to the intersection with a friend; she turned to go to her home just across the street from the school. But my plan was to walk to Daddy's job so I could ride home with him. Just a mile or two on city streets. But Charlie, my classmate, told me to come to her house and wait for Daddy to pick me up there. She said there was no need for me to walk to the store, just come to her house and wait for Daddy there. Charlie is a female and white, which I note here just so you can get a sense of the wonderful people in my town. The sense of sharing, respect, goodness, and kindness was exhibited more than anything else with people living there then, and to this very day. So, I went to Charlie's house and made arrangements for Daddy to come there. Charlie's mother asked me if I wanted anything to eat, or a snack. She also said that she knew my parents, and that they were very kind people.

Chapter 7:
After Dr. Martin Luther King and President John Kennedy; Taylorsville High School

As I noted before this, my new school after the integration policies was Taylorsville High School. The town's Board of Education refused to use that term "integration" and instead chose the term "consolidation." Their policy was not to make it a racial directive, but one where "all students would be affected." The board closed some schools in Alexander County and merged others into separate districts altogether. As a result, I found that many of the students I knew from Happy Plains now lived in different school districts. Those students that I mentioned earlier now attended a school near their homes, which meant no more long bus rides to Taylorsville High before the crack of dawn for them. And they told me that they loved it, loved the school and the people who taught there. When I learned of this plan, I was not certain how it would work out, but it did. The school board also got rid of school mascots. Taylorsville still had the "Cougar" mascot, but other schools had to remove their mascots and vote on another name due to the fact that their mascots were not acceptable for the new era we were entering.

I played basketball there as I had done at Happy Plains High. At this time in my junior year, I noted that in all my classes that I was enrolled in, I was the only black, one of one, present. In the home group class, my friend Polly Parson and I were the only black students. I wondered about this. After a while, I stopped off to ask one of the teachers that I liked there why that was the case. She told me quite frankly that since I had grown up in an all-white neighborhood, and that my parents were respected in our town, that a decision was made for me to integrate with other white students, since I was used to living with them. That would make the white students more comfortable, I was told. That, and with my upbringing, would make the white students less intimated. The school administrators and teachers knew us and our parents. They, the school, also felt that I could handle that situation. I thought that was wonderful. I was helping the "cause," as my parents reared me, and that Dr. Martin Luther King had said to do: to "be at peace" with all men. And as she rightly said, I was used to being with everyone and anybody at any level whether poor, middle class, or wealthy.

Dr. King was on the television during this time in the 1960s. Mama and Daddy were sure to gather us and we saw him on television if there was any news. And there was a lot of news at that time because of the civil rights marches and sit-ins he led. As a child in the elementary school at that time and with our parents, we watched President John F. Kennedy too as he led our country as the youngest President ever elected. Sadly, we also watched when he was murdered in Dallas, Texas. It occurred while I was still in school. When we got home, the television was on. We watched later as his body lay in the Rotunda of the Capitol, and his funeral. We as a family were heartbroken, and remained in shock as the assassination was investigated. Nothing like that had ever happened in our country, and we believed the nation was inconsolable during that period.

Then a few years after President Kennedy's assignation, we watched in horror the news of Dr. Martin L. King being assassinated in Memphis, Tennessee. He was standing on the balcony of a motel. He and his fellow leadership were planning on marching the next day with the garbage collectors for more pay. The crews were predominately black in those days in the South. But after Dr. King was shot, nothing could console us. Mama said that she had been given a word from the Lord about Dr. King, Rev. King, at that time in his actions. As he spoke about "seeing the mountaintop" the previous evening, Mama said she heard from the Lord that he was going to die soon. She said his face had a particular look on it the night of that speech, a kind of sheen.

And when we thought that no other shoe could drop, President Kennedy's brother Robert Kennedy was murdered. All this and the demonstrations against the Vietnam War made me think that our country had changed forever. We were a nation in chaos. None of this, however, changed anything in our neighborhood. In fact, most of us there and in nearby communities were all feeling the same despondence and helplessness. We went on as usual.

As a family, we received special treatment sometimes, mainly because Daddy and Mama were always helping other people throughout the community and town. As for growing up in an all-white neighborhood, I gained an advantage of knowing people who were wealthy and a few who were very wealthy. I, my siblings, and anyone who were living with us at the time learned from my parents how to act in public. They taught us how to respect others, and not to pre-judge people. How to speak and eat properly and what utensils to use, how to cook food and/or serve food to company, sew a button back on a shirt or stitch socks. How to dress appropriately. How to have conversations, either to begin one or to keep one going by showing interest and not feigning interest—mainly because people were interesting, and you could learn a lot about people by listening instead of talking all the time. Friendships were long and deep. Our parents wanted us to know how to maintain a household, whether with a wife or husband, or if you lived alone in a home.

Daddy and Mama did the same things, and I saw this with my own eyes as I grew up. I also learned that, after I graduated from high school, that a job was given to me due in part because of Mama's consent, and as the manager told me, "We are trying to integrate our workers." He continued, "And you grew up with white people, so we want to use you in a slot to start the process." So, needing the money for college in the fall after I graduated from high school, I did start the job. I was placed as an inspector, a job that I was told people worked themselves into. My brothers and my mom worked for this company for many years in the past. It had been the first job out of high school for my brothers Pee, Jim, and Buster. But they had since moved on before my arrival there. I remember them coming home for lunch, though, as the plant was just a short ride home. They too had been put in the section where mostly whites were placed. I believe it was for the same reason given to me. They worked "on the line," and I never heard a complaint from them about conditions. But I was placed as an inspector of the product once it had been put together, not a line worker. So, when I arrived for day one, I soon found myself running into a beehive of hatred.

When coming down the finishing line to inspect the chairs at Broyhill Furniture, the workers on the line would not look at me. Some spat behind me at where I had just stepped. One incident I had encountered happened as I walked to my car at lunchtime. A group of all white men sat at the gate. I knew what was about to happen, but I was not about to let them know that I feared them, which I didn't. As I approached them, one of the men spat at me as I walked past. He worked on my line of employees. Instead of continuing, I turned around and faced the group of men. I stared straight at the one man who had spat at me, and then the group. I stared at them, basically telling them with my expression that said "don't mess with me." And the look also included a dare that if either of them touched me, that I wasn't about to run like a coward, and they would have a fight. Since none of them said any more to me after I stared at them for a while, I turned to continue my walk to my car.

Those men were the same men whose product items I had to inspect. I had always said "good morning" to everyone on the line and anyone else I encountered, even though I received few responses. But gradually, the line began to say "good morning" back to me. From there, that line of men and I began to have contact and really talk. They wanted me to come sit with them at lunch. In fact, the very man who had spat at me as I passed by his position, and had spat at me outside, walked up to me one day in the plant. I was on my break, sitting outside with my mom and her coworkers. The line group I inspected sat away from us at a distance. Upon my return to the line, the man who had once spat at me but no more approached me and said loudly, "If anyone says anything to you that's mean, you let me know! I'll take care of them!" He spat again, away from me that time, and walked off. I had no trouble from him or anyone after that.

I was very happy that those wonderful men and I formed a deep friendship. I remember them to this day as being protective of me. The men were sad to see me go. One said that "just when we were getting to know you, you leave us." That made me sad, because I felt the same way. I was and truly am still glad to this day that God allowed me to have that season with them at Broyhill. It was the first time I had experienced prejudice, yet we all came out the winners and dear friends.

Chapter 8:
Fertile grounds

As I said before, the town of Taylorsville is situated in an area of North Carolina called the Piedmont region. Some memories have stood out more than any others. I don't know why, but this episode stuck with me. Probably because of Daddy's genius. The area was, at that time, known for growing a lot of tobacco and some cotton. I remember having seen these kinds of fields growing up as a youngster. I saw my dad growing tobacco in the field on Daddy's fourteen-acre ancestral property. That was after Mama had gotten a job picking it alongside other women in a field in town. That area has changed and doesn't look that way now.

This occurred during my semi-older years of age nine through ten. I remember seeing the tobacco field my Daddy was planting for us to harvest. He had a bucket filled with white pellets. That turned out to be fertilizer. He was throwing these pellets along a row that he had plowed a few days before, which was now ready for this step. He took a small handful of these tiny pellets and would fling them outward with a sweep of his hand while holding the bucket in the other hand. I watched for a while and asked him if I could try to do that. Daddy was always interested when we were interested in what he was doing. He gave me the instructions of how to use a sweeping motion with one hand to spread the fertilizer across the beige dirt. I tried and succeeded as he had instructed. He smiled and took over the operation. I watched him for a while longer, but the field was pretty large, and I became interested in other things and left him to it.

Later that year I returned to that field with Daddy. Upon arrival I saw that the field had transformed into a field of beautiful and fully developed tobacco leaves! It looked so pretty and full of life. Not a blemish or bug infestation to be seen anywhere on the leaves. "Silkworms" were doing their business. The leaves had grown so high and were waving in the breeze of a warm afternoon. I jumped with surprise and happiness at what those small seeds had produced while I looked over the expanse of the field. The thought came to me that now Mama can come and pick our own tobacco leaves.

I asked Daddy what was next after picking the tobacco. He said we would take it to a barn over nearby, and place it on sticks and tie the leaves to it. Then we would place the wooden sticks, suspended from the rafters, for it to cure and dry in the cabin. I asked where the tobacco barn was. He took me to the woods that surrounded the field. There I saw the small cabin that Daddy had built to house the tobacco. I'd never noticed it before. It apparently had been there all along, though. I never got to see the harvesting of the tobacco, but I am sure that the appearance changed after it had dried.

I have seen documentaries on the way to harvest tobacco since. The sticks are taken down from the rafters, placed lying flat on a burlap cloth, and then sold at auction by auctioneers. The leaves had turned a light golden brown and the bidders walked down a row looking for the best color and texture of each batch on the floor. Daddy had said that money could be made in growing and selling tobacco. I just wondered how he could do this with a full-time job. However, it was satisfying to me that Mama wouldn't ever have to stand tying tobacco to sticks. Mama never did that type of work during the summer after that again.

I watched how Mama and Daddy always honored God and gave Him great respect in their decision making for all of us in the family. I learned from them at an early age that God is just. As part of God's family, He has formed our lives to conform to His. He cares for us and understands the pain and suffering we face. He honors our wishes and our desires to please Him. God never fails or falters, and picks us up when we do. He meets our every need in ways that can be foreign to us, but makes sure that we get His meaning to what happens to us in our lives. Remember, His goodness and light shines in each and every one of us who belong to Him and are His children. We repent, and He keeps us on the straight and narrow in most cases as we may stumble and fall, or fail.

His reach is enormous. His dreams come true for our lives, because He is our destiny on this earth. And it is He who puts the dreams in us, designed them especially unique for us. He guides us, and protects us from all that may be harmful when we are open to His grace. He restores our soul, and makes our lives better for all that occurs both good and evil. He controls our fate, and He minds the small things. Be aware that He also cautions us to be fair to others in all things, and pray for those that may not be that way with us.

We are God's family, His children, and the sheep of His pasture. No one comes to the Father except through the Son. We are made in His image, and we prosper in ways that would astonish those who don't know His son Jesus. He is our great God. No one comes to our Heavenly Father without respect to God's son, however, Jesus the Messiah.

Chapter 9:
Come the holidays: Thanksgiving and Christmas. "For Me and my house, we will serve the Lord."

Joshua 24:15 New King 15: "And if it seems evil to you to serve the Lord, choose for yourselves this day whom you will serve, whether the gods which your fathers served that were on the other side of [a]the River, or the gods of the Amorites, in whose land you dwell. But as for me and my house, we will serve the Lord."

Eating out as family on a Sunday in 2012

Our holidays were celebrated with joyful love, food, gifts, and the ease of those days. Daddy was sent on a mission every year to get a Christmas tree from the land. Now normally he had already spotted which Christmas tree he wanted to cut. Mama loved decorating the tree. And as a young child, I wanted to decorate the tree too. So, Mama would allow me to hang an ornament or two, as I was still young. She placed the tree in the living room. That's the room where guests would come and visit. We had a separate room for the den, where we sat and watched television. The kitchen was nearby, and very handy for a run during commercial breaks. Mama and Daddy's bedroom was off the kitchen area.

At Christmas, when we all lived there as siblings, we looked forward to all the baked goods like cakes and pies. Mama made these from scratch every year. I watched as I was curious as to how she made them. Daddy brought in sacks of oranges, tangerines, candy, all kinds of nuts: a bounty of treats.

I had turned seven or eight years old, and it was Christmastime; I was eagerly waiting as usual for Santa Claus. My brothers and sister were old enough that the season was more adult for them. My little brother Junior and I still believed in Santa Claus. Our parents allowed us to go through the Spiegel and Sears & Roebuck shopping catalogs to look for toys. He and I also yelled out as we sat in front of the television for toys we wanted off the screen. Now Mama and Daddy would ask as we neared Christmas to pick out what we wanted for Santa to bring. We only had a few choices to make, and a parameter had already been set as to how much each of us could ask for and get. Even so, we both ended up getting everything that we asked for with few exceptions.

One toy I had asked for was a teaching doll that would sit in a school chair. I had never asked for a doll before. But I remember this one in particular. It spoke and said words. The doll sat in a chair similar to a classroom. I do remember trying to teach it my elementary school lessons. But she just sat there with that stony face and stared ahead without any interest in me whatsoever. So, I thought, *What was I thinking in asking for this doll?! It is no fun; it doesn't walk or move really easy.* Then I realized just how much my Mama knew me as her child and my play preferences. As I am sure she knew, I would and did lose interest in it. She later gave the doll away to another child, to whom I am certain made good use of it.

Junior finally got his red sleigh for Christmas! The talk of the family was that he got the sleigh he had dreamed of for so long. He showed his excitement in his usual way, much as he does now. A tiny smile creased his lips. He stared at it in disbelief. His eyes went back and forth, just taking it all in, looking and staring over and over again. Then the hands on one hip, a slight step back with the look of approval, and then another smile came on his face, a little deeper this time. The sleigh had brought him so much satisfaction. Now all we needed was some snow! And it came down, right on time.

During the time at home, the winter storms came as predicted or not. Some surprise storms would pepper our city. I really always expected snow for Christmas. I loved snow when it appeared during wintertime, but especially during Christmas. Even if snowed days before and left some powder just to look at, that was fine with me and some of our family. I, Mama, and Daddy seemed to be the biggest fans. Mama or Daddy would call me, even after I had moved away, to tell me that it was snowing outside. I would scream in disappointment that I couldn't be there. Instead, I was here in San Diego, California. My heart broke many times in that moment on the telephone.

When it snowed, the first thing my dad would do was to go out and get the John Deere or other tractor. He would scrape our driveway of snow. Then he would clear the snow with a tractor using a blade at Carolyn's driveway. Then, he would clear up the snow in our church parking lot using the tractor so we could get in to have church that Sunday. My dad's plowing took away the excuse of some to not show up at church that day. In my lifetime living at home, I can only remember a few Sundays where it was too cold for anyone to venture out of doors on a Sunday morning after a snowy weather and deepening temperatures, no matter if the lot had been scraped or not.

You see, Mama and Daddy were always helping people from all over the town and county with problems or advice, doing neighborly things like helping with their children by sending us if the parent needed to go to the doctor. Or Mama would cook for someone who was ill and "shut in" and alone. What she cooked was great looking and tasty—too much so, to my chagrin, as these items went out the door instead of staying on the range top. Oh well. I was left with the wonderful smell of a meal for someone else's house. Begging did nothing to stop the food from being shared with the intended family.

I am very proud of the opportunities provided to us as a family by our parents, and the examples they set for us to follow. Mama and Daddy put themselves out to the community in ways some people or believers would shun. Again, many times strangers would end up in the kitchen sitting at the table with us as we grew up. There is one mystery that occurred that we talked about among ourselves, as told by our mother. One night, the siblings heard a knock at the front door, even though no one who knew us well would come to the front porch of the house. This is the way it was described to me:

Mama heard a knock at the front door. Now only the Hinshaws or strangers ever knocked at the front door. Practically everyone we knew always entered at the back of the house, where they could park their cars and have easier access to the house. But Mama said that when she opened the door, a well-dressed woman stood in front of her. Mama asked her if she was okay and if she needed something. Mama said she didn't answer her questions. Mama invited the woman into the house to rest. Later on, Mama and Daddy invited her to dine with us for the evening meal. She did, but still did not give out any information about herself or why she was out in the night alone. Well, after dinner, Mama said the woman sat there for a while, and then without a word, rose up and left the house. Afterwards no one heard from her or could identify her when Mama and Daddy asked around the neighborhood telling the people about the incident. They were both hoping to find out if she was still safe and had gotten to her destination. Later on, I overheard Mama talking to Daddy about the Bible verse that extols us to treat a stranger well because you may just be entertaining an angel.

KJV Hebrews 13:2 says:

"Be not forgetful to entertain strangers: for thereby some have entertained angels unawares."

Mama and Daddy "entertained" a number of people from the community and those who were passing through who would come to visit. Now this was true entertainment in that they offered her a place to stay if she needed it. She didn't, and continued to her journey down the highway. Mama and Daddy were very concerned that she chose that action, but they had to let her go. But she was talked about among the siblings.

Chapter 10:
The more, the merrier, at times...

Mama and Daddy also allowed the children of Mama's sister, Anna Belle Williams, to live there after she had passed away. Now Mildred and Wilma lived with us. So, there was seven plus two. Later on, two more men came to live there on a long-term basis, Sterling and Ronnie. Sterling was the son of whom I came to call "Aunt Beck" (Rebecca). Aunt Beck had Sterling and a daughter. But the daughter, Alice, stayed with Aunt Beck at her house. Now Sterling's time of stay was spotty at best. He was in and out. Others came and stay for long periods who weren't relatives too at the Mayes home.

All told, according to our family historian—Bettye, our oldest sibling—Mama and Daddy had over forty-seven persons who either had lived there for a long period of time, like Mill and Wilma, or who had stayed over the space of years until they married.

An article was written in the *Taylorsville Times* titled "Mayes couple celebrates 60th wedding anniversary" (June 5, 1996).

2-wheel drive cars. His department did not have any four-wheel drive units. He recalled that tire chains were difficult to find after the first or second storm.

1960, following the winter storms which dumped some 30 inches of snow and sleet over a 33-day period. Photo shows the newspaper office behind the large pile of snow.

1960 scene on Hwy. 90 East of Taylorsville. Howard L. Mayes and Lee Sharpe get a tow behind this 1949 Chevrolet with 'Ole Smokey' along for the excursion.

The hosts were we siblings, but our oldest sister Bettye Lackey directed the entire event. Hundreds of people came out for the event, and the *Taylorsville Times* owner and editor, Lee Sharpe, chronicled the occasion. Lee was a favorite of our Mama and Daddy, as his parents were great friends. My mom told me about seeing him grow up in our neighborhood, just a walking distance from our own home. As an adult, Lee owned the *Taylorsville Times* and was its editor. Excerpts from the paper documented the number and the names of the "over fifty" who had "stayed for a period of one year and more." I will list some of them here:

Ronnie Howell, deceased

Sterling Primus

Bobby McCurdy and children

Wilma Williams (Howell)

Mildred (Mill)

Angela Mayes

Harvey Mayes III

In addition to these cares, both of them had the seven of us to rear, and it never interfered with any of us siblings. In fact, we were the better for it.

I was in grammar school while the other siblings were entering or in high school or college. To say it was a busy household over time is saying the truth. It was busy and crowded with people coming and going: friends dropping by to see one of my siblings, or people who needed to speak to "Harve" for help or advice on important decisions they needed to make. The phone rang "off the hook," according to my mother. And she was right. The telephone rang like a business office phone would. Mama and Daddy always prayed to God for provision and medical treatment for us and whoever was staying with us at that time. Those prayers, from what I have seen, were answered, considering how that house worked. She scrubbed and cleaned up after all of us, and made three meals a day for us to eat.

The investigation by our older sibling Bettye on our ancestry and counting the names of people who still lived in the area points to the fact that they fed and gave shelter over long periods of time to at least forty-seven people. The Lord God always supplied for us, via donations from those in our local community who wanted to help out, or discounted grocery runs because of my parents' involvement in helping so many people. Mama and Daddy were considered to be honest, kind, gentle, and patient. These were characteristics that came naturally to them, as they were blessed by God living in their hearts of mercy.

One of my brother Jim's friends stayed with us occasionally. His name was Terry. I noticed that my brother seemed really concerned about him. I'd never seen my brother be so tender in heart toward anyone else. But he soon learned that Terry was a troubled soul, and Jim and our parents were really worried about him. I don't know who his parents were. Mama and Daddy allowed him to stay with us to try to ease his soul and restore him to happiness and a feeling of worth and well-being.

When I saw Terry, who would come on some overnight stays, he looked sad. He had sadness on his face all the time. He seemed to be troubled about something. Nevertheless, our family welcomed him in as part of us and because Jim wanted to help him. I didn't see Terry after that short time period. But what happened next rocked Jim to his very core.

Apparently, Terry couldn't cope with what was tormenting his soul. One sad day, he sat on train tracks. The engineer saw him and blew his horn to make Terry move off the tracks. But the engineer said that he wouldn't move. He kept blowing the train whistle and couldn't stop in time to avoid hitting Terry. He had committed suicide. This devastated Jim. He was distraught and shocked. He had tried to help Terry, and thought he had made progress. I asked Jim why Terry did this deliberately. He just looked away. Mama and Daddy told the family later that Terry had always said that he wanted to die. He didn't want to live any longer.

The funeral was at his mother's home. I didn't know her name, but she was distraught. I saw him lying there in the casket with his mom sobbing seated beside him. I had debated whether to go in and see him. I had never seen a body in a casket before. My mom assured me it would be okay if I wanted to go and look at him or not. I did. He was expressionless. His eyes were closed, and his face looked strained. I didn't know if the fact that he was hit by a train contributed to the way he looked. I would not look at the body in the casket at other funerals for years to follow.

In one story after another, our mom and dad—through God and lots of prayer—kept us all fed and taught us the word of God in action on a daily basis. I remember one story as told to me by Mama, that Sarah Mae, Ronnie, and O'Neil Jr. his little brother mother, stayed with on our fourteen-acre property, but used their own mobile home. There was a period in Sarah life when she entered the employ of the Hinshaws. She was paid very well after she negotiated with Mr. Hinshaw. She cooked and cleaned the house. In the past before I was born, Mama told me that a couple of Hinshaw's maids stayed at Mama and Daddy's house. As I said before, the Hinshaws, Daddy's employer, made an agreement whereby my mother and father could stay there rent free. Thus, for a few months or so upon her arrival from "up north," Sarah Mae lived in our house alone among our siblings. Hinshaw let the single help stay there for a while, usually until other situations could be discovered. She moved out, however, after a short time there, and went back to a northern state where she could get better pay and take advantage of the market of doing more than just houses. She became a nurse after a while.

But as I had said before, her son Ronnie stayed in North Carolina with our family as his preference. He didn't like living in the big cities, nor what he had to put up with in the way of challenges from the neighborhoods there. Sarah herself felt he would be safer with Mama and Daddy in the South. Morals were followed and there was no peer pressure to follow bad influences in the city. At that time, Sarah had married a man named O'Neil, and eventually she did return to the South. She had been diagnosed with cancer, and wanted to come home. She asked Mama and Daddy if they could be with us. But instead, a mobile home was placed there that Sarah had purchased on the fourteen acres of land owned by Mama and Daddy for her family. Now their son O'Neil Jr. and daughter Lucille could live along with her husband O'Neil Sr. Sarah did pass away, leaving her children with their father. Eventually the family moved to South Carolina, where his family had a base.

Our home played host to others as I said before, within and out of our family relatives. As Mama and Daddy's deeds grew and after multiple decades of showing the love of God to not only us, but to others, the town awarded them multiple honors upon honors. They were put in the hometown Christmas parade as honorees due to their selfless work in ours and other towns surrounding our town's communities. They were known and honored by countless people who had been given hope, a home, or repairs! Daddy was constantly helping people.

The *Taylorsville Times* also noted his contribution to the community, as the Alexander County Chamber of Commerce voted and honored Daddy with the title "1999 Alexander County Citizen of the Year." *The Taylorsville Times* said that the chamber's director, Keith Hertzier, knew Mayes wouldn't show up to collect his own award. She added, "See, he doesn't like to be recognized for anything." She continued, "We told him that—let's see, what did they tell him? That his church was going to get an award, and that the church wanted him to go and accept the award. So, he just came in there and sat there quietly and then, at the end, found out what it was all about.... He was very surprised." The article goes on to say, "Church members and other community leaders, including Town Manager George Holleman and last year's winner Richard Walker, nominated Mayes for the award given annually to an Alexander County resident who's made significant contributions to community life." The article itself is inserted here:

rvey Mayes has fed the hungry and housed the temporarily homeless in this small farmhouse in Taylorsville for decades. For
s devotion to community and church, he's been named the Alexander County Citizen of the Year.

Heart, soul, service

Alexander County honors 84-year-old man

"I guess I'm proud of it, but . . . I feel I'm not worthy of it. All this earthly praise don't do you much good."

HARVEY MAYES
ON BEING NAMED CITIZEN OF THE YEAR

By GREG LACOUR
Staff Writer

TAYLORSVILLE — Harvey Mayes could barely see.

It was dark outside, the kind of enveloping dark you get in a little country town at night. Mayes, fresh off a full day's work in his hay and corn fields, was here, trying to rebuild the church he loved after his own brother had accidentally burned it to the ground.

He worked by lantern — electricity hadn't made it to Taylorsville in 1942 — and inched along, beam by beam in the darkness a few dozen feet from the church's small cemetery until the subflooring was finished.

It took him several months.

"I was scared at night, too," he said, 57 years later. "I was

scared of them dead people."

The church, Macedonia Baptist Church on, N.C. 90, rose again, largely because of Mayes. Today, as then, he's a lean man with bright, brown eyes and skin the color of chestnuts, although age and disease has taken a toll.

Time hasn't diluted his love of his church and community, though. He cherishes the church so much and attention for himself so little, in fact, that the Alexander County Chamber of Commerce had to lie to him.

The chamber had decided that the 84-year-old Mayes would be the 1999 Alexander County Citizen of the Year and planned to give him the award at its 48th annual meeting last month. But chamber executive

director Keith Hertzler knew Mayes wouldn't show up to collect his own award.

"See, he doesn't like to be recognized for anything," Hertzler said last week. "We told him that — let's see, what did they tell him? — that his church was going to get an award, and that the church wanted him to go and accept the award. So he just came in there and sat there quietly and then, at the end, found out what it was all about.

"Oh, yes," Hertzler said, chuckling. "He was very surprised."

Church members and other community leaders — including Town Manager George Holle-

See MAYES / *page* 10V

55

FROM THE COVER

Alexander County honors 84-year-old Taylorsville man

MAYES *from 1V*

man and last year's winner, Richard Walker — nominated Mayes for the award, given annually to an Alexander County resident who's made significant contributions to community life.

Mayes works hard for the community, the nominations said, and helps his neighbors whenever they need it.

Over the 63 years Mayes and his wife, Lucille, have lived together in Taylorsville, they've fed anyone who's needed a meal. They still drive some of their elderly friends, some younger than they, to doctor's appointments when the friends can't.

The Mayeses live in the same cramped but well-kept two-story farmhouse they've lived in for decades, and Mayes has allowed neighbors and acquaintances to sleep there when they've needed.

Often, he'd wake up before dawn on cold mornings to find people he barely knew sleeping before the fireplace.

They usually were white, too. The Mayeses were the only black family in the neighborhood for years, but Mayes said he experienced discrimination only in the towns and cities he drove to on his job delivering goods to stores.

"But not out here in the country," said Mayes' daughter Bettye Lackey, 59, of Statesville. "It was like we were equal out here in the country."

Mayes balanced others' fair treatment with his own hard work.

He once ordered a hospital where he was awaiting surgery for throat cancer to release him so he could supervise the pouring of a new concrete walkway for the church, where he's a deacon; he

JEFF WILLHELM/Staff

Helping rebuild Macedonia Baptist Church is the kind of deed that led Harvey Mayes to be named Alexander County Citizen of the Year.

thought no one else had time to do it. When the concrete was poured, he went back to the hospital.

All those years earlier, he'd been happy to help rebuild the church. His brother, Ted, was a deacon and Sunday-school superintendent, and he dropped in early one cold Sunday morning to light the old, pot-bellied stove for the Sunday-school class.

He left, the fire sparked onto wooden shingles, and the place went up.

"We didn't have no water, didn't have no ladder to get up there, didn't have no phone to call anybody," Mayes said. "So we just let it burn."

Ask him if he's proud of his award, though, and he winces.

"To tell you the truth, it makes me feel bad," he said last week. "I guess I'm proud of it, but . . . I feel I'm not worthy of it. All this earthly praise don't do you much good."

The cancer and surgery, in 1985, took some of Mayes' vitality. Surgeons removed part of his jaw, and he has trouble talking. He's suffered from gout for the past de-

cade, too, and walks painfully, with a cane.

The doctors told him they might have to amputate one or both of his legs because the circulation to his feet was so bad.

"I wouldn't let 'em," Mayes said.

Instead, they inserted a tube in one leg and plan the same for the other.

Still, Mayes hurts. He doesn't complain, though. He says he gets strength from the Bible, which he couldn't read until his mid-50s. One of his granddaughters was reading "The Three Little Pigs," and Mayes decided he'd better learn to read in case she ever asked him to read to her.

So he attended adult-education classes at what was then Taylorsville High School.

"I was proud to get to go," he said. "But I never was into that book-learning. I learned about the little red hen and the sky is falling, but I had no use for that.

"I learned to read the Bible, the first book of the Bible, Matthew, and I was happier with that than I was with anything in the world."

56

Mama and Daddy (Miss Lucille and Uncle Harve) receiving another award. This one is the Man of the Year award from their county head commissioner.

Later in the following years, Lee was requested by Mama and Daddy to come to Macedonia Baptist Church, which was having an event honoring her on her ninety-second birthday. The event included our family photo in the paper with her in the center, smiling with joy as we surrounded her. Our mom's sister, Nellie, and her children were included, as we had actually grown up together in the same house.

Chapter 11:
Love of Sundays

As a child, and I dare say as adults too, we really enjoyed living at home with my parents and siblings. We were happy growing up there. Lots of people in the town told us how lucky we were to have "Harve" and "Lucille" for our mom and dad. Or they used "Uncle Harve" and "Miss Lucille" more often than not.

One day as a child, I looked out from the back screen door. I observed one of my favorite scenes: the brick well house. The day was sunny and clear, not a cloud in the sky. I was very happy and smiled. I love that well house. As a child, I played around it often. It's dark, but not too dark, with shafts of light peering through the cracks, and always comfortable and dry. Even in heavy rain and snow. Mama put canned fruit in the other shed too for our winter eating. But when she first learned the art of preserving food, the well house was the first step for her.

Mama had grown up in a struggling family who had to walk to a lake to draw water for their house in buckets. Perhaps in the summer that was nice, but not in the worst of winter with temperatures below zero. And as Mama told me, having to walk two miles one way, the chore was more like hardship. I remembered her words as I gazed at the jars and other items in the well house. These shelves held some of Mama's jar food on them. Now Mama, one year during the bounty season of fruit and veggies, saw her placing the jars in the shed near my brother's barbershop. We did eat the food stored there the following year. It appeared to me that God always gave us more than we normally preserved. Like an overflow.

I remember that because I had to get used to going into that shed sometimes to get jars. In fact, when I actually went there, I had to steel myself against nightmares of spiders lurking in hidden sectors. Never saw or found one. Not one. Some of Daddy's tools lay in the next section. Some things were important like tools Daddy used, but mostly old and not needed items were stored. But that day, I was on my way to church. Macedonia Baptist Church.

Daddy was a deacon there and a steward. A steward is important because they are put in charge of counting the offerings and making sure it gets to the bank. Mama was the director of the church choir. She led a Bible study at home once a week. On Sundays, Mama would put beautiful dresses on me and my sister Mary, one of the ones I wore only for church days. My socks were white with lace trim. Mostly the norm. My dress was frilly too with its white collars. All little children had this type of dress. I was six years old at that point. And I loved this day, Sunday. We all dressed up in our finest clothing, hats, and gloves if you were older. Hats, suits, and stockings were worn by the wives and ladies. Three-piece suits on the guys, and Daddy with his hat. So beautiful. So pretty. So handsome, my brothers and father.

The scenario went like this. Daddy was about to come and pick us up for church. He was already at church, making sure that all was in order for Pastor Moore and the members. Pastor Moore was from out of town. Daddy always waited on him, to be certain that his needs were met with perfection. Daddy was a servant of the Highest God and served Rev. Moore with pleasure. They were really good friends off the pomp and circumstance of protocol. Rev. Moore stayed at our house often. Sometimes he would even spend a night there in the guest room if he was too tired to drive home—a good forty-five-minute drive on dark country roads. If we had all-day services, he ate with our family, and lay down in the bedroom at the front of the house to rest before the next service.

Now, when we had our "church conferences," the Sunday outfits went to another level when we were adults. My brothers all had their new suits, because it was a meeting of multiple churches, and all wanted to look their best. My sister Mary and her high school friends dressed in suits as well. But Mary had asked her brothers to take her to another town to purchase suits for her on this occasion. It only happened once, because clothing then was well made and she could wear them for years. She came back with three new suits that were beautiful to me. And since she had gone out of town to buy them, no one could have the same ones.

She had her Sunday morning service suit. After that, she came home and changed into her afternoon church suit ensemble for the sermon of the afternoon guest speaker. Then she had her evening suit, and shoes to all of these of course, for the evening church services. I shall never forget that day. I was so very much impressed with her and how she appeared, as were quite a few others at church. The elders or seniors gave her wide complements on her outfits. As did her close friends. That pleased her. I don't even remember what I had on. But I am certain Mama and Daddy had me covered in the best as well, as usual for all of us.

You see, Sundays were when you wore your best outfit, no matter how many times you wore it. Ensembles included hats, gloves, a suit, and shoes. For men, hats and suits. That was the norm for our region of the world, the Southeast. Didn't matter if you were at any other church, as that was the norm for their congregations too. We dressed our best for God, because we wanted to honor Him for the blessings he had given all of us. And He had blessed us to be able to purchase food and clothing for our family. We also tithed ten percent of our income to the church as well.

In addition, my dad was always repairing things, mowing the grass, in general being the caregiver to the building. In fact, after a while, the church voted to pay him fifty dollars a week for this, because he had done it on his own for decades. The boys would help on occasion, just as they do now for Macedonia, spending some of their off-work time to support whatever or whomever needed help or repairs there. But! My father refused to take the money, wishing only to honor God with his work. So, the church voted to put the money in the collection to add to the tithes he and Mama always paid. And they taught us to pay as well as we grew up and got jobs.

Chapter 12:
Macedonia, meals, and we loved Sundays

Mama cooked some parts of the Sunday meals on Saturdays. Many times, she would cook meals for us and those who were having hard times feeding their families, including those who were too sick to perform that role for their families. She and Daddy also would buy groceries for others who needed to feed their families. On Sunday mornings, Mama drove around in what she referred to as the "Henry Jay." I remember it well. We all piled into the car, a black car that seated seven, and in which she used to drive the younger ones like me and my little brother to church every Sunday. Or when we met at the church during the week for Bible study at nights during the week.

Daddy used his truck, and if it wasn't raining, the older boys—Jessie, Howard (Pee-Wee) and Jim, rode with him. Otherwise, Mama made two trips to get everyone there. Daddy was the deacon who opened the church up, and got the heating going in the winter. He always left our house very early in the morning to do that, and to make sure the church was ready to receive the large flock of members. He also waited to watch out for our pastor, Reverend Moore, to arrive. Rev. Moore taught the adult Sunday school class. The church was only five minutes away from our house by car. We would all meet "up there" and go in as a family when services started.

This is more like what most Americans grew up with prior to the explosion of the "Now Generation," the disrespect of authority or institutions that had been the basis of civilization for centuries. Music changed, culture changed, people grew apart. Families grew apart. The days of riots and marches in the streets against the United States government grew in intensity and in mass. Drugs were introduced that even to this day inflict death and destruction on adults of all ages. This curse still emanates in our society today, but with even more destructive and deadly results. Religion has been placed on the chopping block by organizations like the American Civil Liberties Union (ACLU) and individual groups such as George Soros. He heads the group called "Open Society." His organization, and that of the ACLU, have proven to many in this country that their agenda is to remove religion from the face of the earth in any form or fashion. Many like them, including elected officials in some states in this pandemic, also work tirelessly to interfere with the viability of the church in America today. Thus disrupting the continuity of the family we once knew and grew up in. Facebook and other social media, including the news itself, has placed the lives of our country in the crosshairs of defeatism. Their goal appears to be to dismantle our private lives. Peer pressure is the main avenue used, as it can affect countless people of all ages.

Peer pressure then was vastly different from peer pressure now. Now you are bullied or shunned if you align yourself with Christians, or dare show that by carrying a Bible with you. You might be singled out by the other students in high school or college for having morals of any kind. In other words, the extent of your belief, per God's standards even if you have not accepted the Messiah, is cause for a teacher to give you a low grade whether deserved or not. These immoral "teachers" or "professors" require class participation in order to learn the views of those in their classrooms. Daunting. Your personal views should not negate your efforts in the classroom of the teacher. Yet most colleges these days hire "professors" who teach whatever the biased administration viewpoint or philosophy is. One way or another, their day is coming where God will hold them personally responsible for their deceit. God has always saved his righteous ones and those who try to do the right thing. Injustice by those in authority is never left unpunished. Just ask Hamon, Og, Sanballat, and Tobias. These were men who attempted to stop any good thing for the Hebrews by going to war against them, including the rebuilding of the wall around Jerusalem.

Nehemiah 4:1-6: "What are these feeble Jews doing? Are they going to restore it for themselves? Can they offer sacrifices? Can they finish in a day? Can they revive the stones from the dusty rubble even the burned ones?" Now Tobias the Ammonite was near him and he said, "Even what they are building—if a fox should jump on it, he would break their stone wall down!" Hear, O our God, how we are despised! Return their reproach on their own heads and give them up for plunder in a land of captivity. Do not forgive their iniquity and let not their sin be blotted out before Thee, for they have demoralized the builders. So, we built the wall and the whole wall was joined together to half its height, for the people had a mind to work."

Like those that opposed King David, there were just as many men and women who were vindicated by Yeshua for their destiny to continue. Just remember, the memory of those who sin in authority will fade, but not from God's eye. Nor from the *Book of Life*. All people will have a final judgment by Almighty God. And even though as believers, we too will find upon reaching Heaven that some decisions we made in particular to candidates for election will be corrected. In other words, those believers who loosely or casually approached life with their own philosophy instead of the biblical standards based on God's word will see an ungodly perspective of this world plunge even deeper into chaos. And if decisions about those in authority over us are not based in the word of God, but based on their philosophy or what that person "thinks" about what God "meant," they will reap the whirlwind of those decisions on earth. Bank on it. It still wouldn't be the first time a nation turned away from God. Read the book of Jeremiah, and see the reflection there of what is currently going on in this nation and others. God always wins.

I wrote a poem to honor Daddy, which was read in the church, called "Wo Daddy Wo." The poem was about when he and Mama were being honored by the members of Macedonia for all the hard work they had done for the church, all the work and help that they were doing for the members and the work throughout the community. Many community leaders and the mayor of town, Elvis Barringer, came with gifts. Mama and Daddy, I was told by the mayor, raised him when he was in need of help. To that point, after he married, the mayor would arrive every Thanksgiving with a ham for Mama and Daddy, even after Daddy had passed away. I know this to be true, because Mayor Barringer told me this in our backyard one day, how Mama and Daddy had saved him. He didn't go into details, but he was clearly moved by the experience. Mrs. Barringer (Jackson) turned out to be my basketball coach at Taylorsville High School, by the way. Yes, she is just as kind and good as the mayor. So, I wrote this poem to honor them, as I couldn't be there.

Daddy Wo:

Wo Daddy! Wo!
Came the urgent cry.

Can I go! Can I go!
Her Hope
Rising with each little step,
Toward the man in full stride.

"Maybe next time," came the reply.

Disappointment crushed through her.
Some tears almost appeared.
Oh Daddy? Why?
But why?
Wondered the little girl who watched,
As the man disappeared into the early morning sunrise.

This scene was repeated.
Through countless Days that bled into
Years.
The little girl listened or watched,
As her Daddy Disappeared.

Then one day, one sunny summer afternoon,
The man who Disappears came into her room and said,
"Come. Come go with me.
Come go with me here."

Eagerly, she climbed into his truck.
The truck he loved so dear.
It was another faithful companion to him,
To the man who Disappeared.

We rode out to the end of the driveway.
Then he turned to the right.
The man who Disappears on me, I thought,

Was about to show me life.

He turned into an unfamiliar driveway.
This was frightening, at first.
But then as he smiled and waited for me,
I felt it okay to leave the safety of my perch.

He approached the foreign people,
And with a smile and a twinkle in his eyes,
I felt his ease and warmth rush through me.
As did the strangers too, melting their fears inside.

"I heard you have some problems,"
The man who Disappears said.
"I've come to help you."
What is it do you need?
How can I help you best?"

The response from the strangers,
Was as swift and precise.
"I can't figure it out Harve."
"Ya got any good advice?"

I watched in amazement,
And was awed, and
Very pleased.

As this man who Disappears,
Worked Confidently.
Reassuringly.

We went on many trips such as these.
Some once, Some twice.
Some took a great deal of expertise.
He gave a lot of advice.

And I finally understood,
And I finally got to see
Why the man who Disappeared on me,
Took flight, with such great ease.

From dawn to dusk, he rose to do,
Those wonderful things his earthy and heavenly Fathers
taught him in his youth.

I watched, and learned, and came to believe.
That the 'Great Commission,'
"To go out and share my life,"
Was never lost on this man.

"If you lift me up, I will draw all men to me"
The man who Disappears, and his wife,
Had done this almost all of their lives.

The number of boarders, who came to stay.
Who brought their problems too.
To many to count. Can't even guess.
Such things never mattered to those two.

The times of sharing the gospel,
With strangers, or with friends.
A meal and a room, and how often
Mom cooked to feed an endless crew.

They have put into action,
Those things God holds so dear,
They have God's Son you see, in their hearts,
"To those who can hear," let them hear."

From a childhood to an adulthood,
Over the years I've come to understand,
The man who Disappeared on me you see,
Was a man with a mission and a plan.

And a mother, who worked just as hard as he,
Tending children,
And even great grandbabies,

Creating for us beautiful, colorful, bountiful things.
Or showing us,
Just how to Be.

Years, not enough time to explain,
No time will allow me to tell.
How they both have changed all our lives
With prayers and advice, until all was well.

"Well done my good and faithful Servants,"
I am CERTAIN they will hear.
The man who Disappeared on me will smile,
Yes, with a twinkle in his eyes,
He'll smile from ear to ear!

©Bessie Mayes 2000

Chapter 13:
Aunt/Miss Lucile and Mama Judy: their legacy

Mama had a very interesting history or lineage. Mama is a direct descendant from a slave woman named Mama Judy.

Her particular link was through a daughter of Mama Judy named Sue. Sue was one of thirteen children born to Mama Judy. The first one was Lucy, followed by Annie, Callie Sue, Laura, Mimia, Mary, Clara, Sue (Mama descended from her line with Ms. Elizabeth Grinton being her cousin), Alice, Martha, Rachel, and Eliza. Eliza, the baby girl of the main branch, had ten children. Mama Judith had a daughter named Sue, who was born the sixth child and had seven of her own. Her children's names were Ellen, Lillie, Judy, Isabelle, Alfred, and Nathan. Ellen had Josephine, who birthed Elizabeth Grinton, the line of my mom's as Elizabeth's cousin.

I talked about my lineage of slavery staring with Mama Judith in a classroom speech project for African-American history at San Diego State University. During break, one student said to me that he had thought that all this talk about slavery was a lie and that he didn't believe this course book. Then he said, holding back tears, "and there you are. A descendant from slavery. Alive. And when you said one had died and no one knew how, I couldn't believe. But here you are, alive and in college, and getting a college degree."

I was stunned. I couldn't respond to his comment because I thought everyone knew the history of slavery, and two, the impact of the report had moved him to tears. I thanked God for that response. I also thanked God because he made me interested enough to travel with my own Mama to speak with Elizabeth Grinton, her cousin. Mama really wanted to know about her lineage. I myself am still impacted to this day about what God did for my mother, and next me. More importantly, what God had done for that young man who now will, in his own words, "see a real person that came from slavery standing before me."

One more thing I noted about Mrs. Grinton's manuscript. One of Mama Judith's children, Eliza, had ten offspring. One was named Bessie. I know my name came from honoring my father's mother, Mom Bessie. I loved that it did. And I also noted that Eliza, the last child of Mama Judith, had also named one of her children Bessie too. And although my brother Jessie's name came from my father, honoring a request from Mr. Hinshaw, his employer, to give Jessie his middle name Milton, it appears that both of our names appear under Eliza's line. Milton was also one of the names Eliza gave to one of her sons. My parents also felt comfortable with the names. The Hinshaws were in no way reflective of the slave era, nor the segregation era in my time. In fact, the mere example of how we were treated and respected by the family showed that the prejudice of that era did not affect our home life.

I wrote an essay for my college class under African Studies. The paper and a presentation were required as part of the class. I put together a large cardboard presentation with Mama Judy at the top, and her children diagramed below her in order of their birth. I took in examples of the area where Mama Judy stayed, like pictures of her cabin. And I had acquired a log of the history of slave ownership in Wilkesboro City and the county area. The presentation was well received. And there were a lot of questions that followed from the class, so it went over the ten minutes of the allotted time. I have put the paper below for you to read.

An Essay on Judith Barber (Mammie Judy); An Ancestral Slave

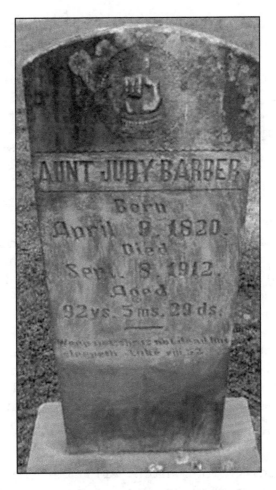

According to the African-American Literature in Context section located in the back of *The Norton Anthology of African Americans*, the year 1820 was an important one for African-Americans. The state of Maine joined the Union as a "free" state, and the American Colonization Society, which had formed in 1816 in Washington, DC, "sends [an] expedition to begin establishment of Liberia, a black republic in West Africa ..." (p. 2613) Eighty-six blacks sailed off on a ship called

Mayflower of Liberia from the docks of New York City to birth another kind of nation into existence. A nation where men and women could once again live as free individuals, no longer under the cruelty of slavery. Unfortunately, slavery was still a thriving part of the America system and American dream. But the next few years would see a birth of another kind. A girl would never completely experience the promising future into which the ship the *Mayflower of Liberia* sailed with its passengers. At the tender age of twelve, she would begin to experience what most black women her age had experienced for many decades prior to her birth, separation from her family, isolation, loneliness, pain, rape, and fear. Attempts to escape from this situation would meet with serious consequences. Instead of a journey ending in freedom in West Africa, this little girl's journey into a "new world" would end in imprisonment and forced labor in the mountains of North Carolina. That twelve-year-old girl was Judith Barber or "Mammy" Judy.

The information which will be presented in this essay on Judith Barber is new. The book *Treasure Troves*, which will be referenced at times in this essay, is at present only available in the manuscript form. The material critiqued in the analysis section of this essay covers only the foreword and the introduction section of the book.

I plan to show how Judith Barber's experiences during her slavery years compare or parallel those of other women in slavery. I will also compare the writing styles between the *True Treasure* author, Elizabeth Grinton, to those of Harriet Jacobs, whose writings I believe were similarly constrained for the comfort of the audience.

Historical Background

According to Elizabeth Grinton, a fifth-generation descendent and the author of *Treasure Troves*, Mammy Judy was born April 9, 1820 in Yadkin County, North Carolina. Her parentage is unknown. Yadkin County had not been formed as a county at the time of Mammy Judy's birth. The county, which formed in 1850, was still a part of Surry County which had formed in 1771 from Rowan County. So, it is very likely that at the time of Mammy Judy's birth, her official place of birth would have been placed in Surry County instead of the present-day Yadkin County.

At the age of twelve, Mammy Judy entered into slavery. Her mistress, Mary Taylor Williams, brought her and one hundred other slaves from Surry County to Wilkes County. According to Grinton from the foreword of *Treasure Troves*, "we, also, verify knowledge of the 'Sale Purchase' place in Surry County, North Carolina - by a Major Joseph Williams of Logtown, Rockford County seat."

I believe that I am correct in assuming that Major Joseph Williams was the father of Mary T. Williams, who was the mistress of Mammy Judy. By owning this many slaves, Mary

T. Williams would have been considered a wealthy individual. No information is available about Mary William's reasons for moving to Wilkes County, or where she stayed upon arrival. However, Wilkes County would now be the permanent home of Mammy Judy and most of her children.

Elizabeth Grinton gives a description of Mammy Judy as an adult in her introduction to *Treasure Troves*. Grinton writes that she was slight in stature, and always wore a black dress, a white apron, and a white skullcap. Mammy Judy received her name Mammy because of one of her responsibilities, that of a mid-wife. She gave birth to thirteen girls, nine of whom lived to maturity. Three died at birth, with one death (see written genealogy chart in packet) at the age of thirteen. No information is available on the circumstances surrounding this death. Mammy Judy "married" or had a companion named Anthony, another slave on the plantation. Mammy Judy and Anthony, as slaves, did not have legal rights as citizens, so were not allowed to marry.

Sometime during her stay in Wilkes County, Mary Williams met and married John P. Peden. Mammy Judy was given the last name of Peden as well. Mr. Peden and his wife Mary had three children. A daughter, Fannie Williams Peden, and two sons, John P. Peden and Joseph William Peden. After the death of John Peden Sr., Mary Peden married again. This time to Richard Barber, the second rector at St. Paul's Episcopal Church.

Richard Barber had moved to Wilkes County for health reasons, leaving his first church in Plymouth (*Genealogy of Wilkes County*, v.1, p. 90). According to Grinton, "Barber" would be the last name change for Mammy Judy, who was given the Master's last name, as well as her children.

As a slave, Mammy Judy worked from day break to dusk, taking care of the children from the first marriage as well as the two new children which would be born to Richard Barber. The Barber children were William Wainwright Barber, born October 14, 1855, and Mary Taylor Barber, born January 6. Grinton describes some of Mammy Judy's duties in the *Genealogy of Wilkes County*, p. 91. She comments that, "while in servitude, she worked as head cook, head launderer, seamstress, nurse maid, and entertainer for the master's children."

Grinton also states that Mammy Judy's own children were also assigned work in the master's home.

"As her daughters grew and worked along beside her, she taught them various chores."

Historically, seven of Mammy Judy's children remained with her on the plantation during her servitude; three died at birth from unknown causes. However, two children, Alice and Martha, were sold by the Richard Barber for an undetermined amount of money.

According to personal accounts from Elizabeth Grinton, Mammy Judy became indispensable to her master, Richard Barber. To show appreciation to her, he had a cabin built, just for her family and Anthony (see figure 1). Grinton comments in *Treasure Troves* that "... the house was kept immaculate."

Mammy Judy and her family worked inside the master's house, never outside like other slaves, and was referred to as the "house nigger."

Some Realities of Slavery; Rape

The life of a slave presented in the preliminary pages of *Treasure Troves* seemed almost idealistic compared to other personal narratives written by slaves. However, it is my opinion that Mammy Judy suffered some of the same traumatic occurrences in her life as another writer in similar circumstances, the author, Harriet Jacobs.

Jacobs, another North Carolinian slave, relived an incident in her true-life narrative, *Incidents in the Life of a Slave*. Jacobs was subjected to constant sexual harassment from Dr. James Norcom (Dr. Flint in *Incidents*). She convinced another white attorney, Samuel Tredwell Sawyer, (Mr. Sands in *Incidents*) to "form a clandestine liaison" to prevent Dr. Norcom from forced sexual intercourse. Her reason being that if Sawyer impregnated her first, Dr. Norcom would stop harassing her. She follows through on her plan, and explains her decision to her readers. She wrote,

But, O, ye happy women,
whose purity has been
sheltered from homes are
protected by law, do not
judge the poor desolate
slave girl of my choice; I
could have had a home
shielded by the laws; and
I should have been spared
the painful task of
confessing what I am now
keep myself pure; and,
under the most adverse
circumstances, I tried
hard to preserve my self-
respect; but I was
struggling alone in the
powerful grasp of the
demon Slavery; and the
monster proved too strong
frustrated; and I became
reckless in my despair.
(*The Norton Anthology of
African American
Literature*, p. 219)

Rape was an act committed continuously on female slaves by the slave masters. This fact has been verified in many writings throughout history. It is my belief too that the first master of Mammy Judy, John Peden, physically assaulted or raped her. Although no legal records are available to confirm this theory, personal accounts from Elizabeth Grinton indicate that the skin color among the thirteen children of Mammy Judy varied considerably. These forced sexual attacks upon female slaves always resulted in the birth of mixed-race children. According to William Wells Brown in one of his stories, *From the Clotel; or, The President's Daughter*, (*The Norton Anthology of African American Literature*) seeing such offspring was common. Mr. Brown, who was himself the seed of a white slave master, relates in *Clotel* the attitude among white society in the south regarding mixed or "mulatto" offspring. He writes,

> With the growing population of slaves in the Southern States of America, there is a fearful increase of half whites, most of whose fathers are slaveowners, and their mother's slaves. Society does not frown upon the man who sits with his mulatto child upon his knee, whilst its mother stands a slave behind his chair. (*The Norton Anthology of African American Literature*, p. 255)

Slaves were not considered human or citizens, and therefore had no legal protection against such attacks. Consequently, slave masters were not held legally responsible for rape among female slaves, as would be the case for rape among white females. From a handout titled Excerpts from U.S. Slave Law, a legal precedent was set in a

Mississippi court of Appeals in 1859 about the crime of rape among slaves. In this argument, we can see the lack of legal protection for the female slave for assault even from other male slaves. In oral arguments in the case of George vs. State, the judge states,

> The crime of rape does
> not exist in this State
> between African slaves.
> Our laws recognize no
> marital rights as between
> slaves … The regulations
> of law, as to the white
> race, on the subject of
> sexual intercourse, do not
> and cannot, for obvious
> reasons, apply to slaves;
> their intercourse is
> promiscuous, and the
> violation of a female
> slave by a male slave
> would be a mere assault
> and battery. (Excerpts
> from U.S. Slave Law)

Additionally, Ida B. Wells-Barnett comments in her *A Red Record* essay about lies and myths told by white abolitionists concerning "Negro" men who were constantly falsely accused of raping white women. She writes,

> In his remarkable
> apology for lynching,
> Bishop Haygood, of
> Georgia, says: "No race,
> not the most savage,

tolerates the rape of
woman, but it may be said
without reflection upon
any other people that the
Southern people are now
and always have been most
sensitive concerning the
honor of their women—their
mothers, wives, sisters
and daughters." It is not
the purpose of this
defense to say one word
against the white women of
the South. Such need not
be said, but it is their
misfortune that the
chivalrous white men of
that section, in order to
escape the deserved
execration (curse) of the
civilized world, should
shield themselves by their
cowardly and infamously
false excuse, and call
into question that very
honor about which their
distinguished priestly
apologist claims they are
most sensitive. To justify
their own barbarism, they
assume a chivalry which
they do not possess. True
chivalry respects all
womanhood, and no one who
reads the record, as it is
written in the faces of
the million mulattoes in

the South, will for a
minute conceive that the
southern white man had a
very chivalrous regard for
the honor due the women of
his own race or respect
for the womanhood which
circumstances placed in
his power. That chivalry
which is "most sensitive
concerning the honor of
women" can hope for but
little respect from the
civilized world, when it
confines itself entirely
to the women who happen to
be white. (*Norton
Anthology of African
Americans*, p. 600)

Wells-Barnett's conclusion was that many
southern white slave masters had little
concern for female slaves. Certainly, for no
other reason but to be used for sexual
gratification, and to keep the profits made
from selling the offspring from these
encounters.

Some Realities of Slavery; Profiting in Human Flesh

Another harsh reality of slavery however
did affect Mammy Judy. She had to accept
painfully that two of her children, Alice and
Martha, while still young children, were sold
as slaves. However, Grinton states that

eventually these two women were returned to Wikes County. A granddaughter of Mammy Judy's, Annie found and returned the body of Alice for burial beside her mother's grave. Martha was also located by Annie and returned to her home town for reburial.

Historically, laws all over the United States considered slaves the property of the slave masters, whether fathered by the slave master or "husband." Consequently, it was common to sell the slaves for profit, just like the slave master would any animal on the plantation. A document from the **Loudoun Company** lists the sell, trade and/or rental of Negro slaves to other participants involved in the slave trade. The document dates from December 13, 1809 to June 30, 1861. A statement from the comment section reads,

> "The 'negro boy Peter'
> was sold for $450. Doesn't
> state who bought him. He
> was sold ... 'in
> conformity to a clause in
> the testator's will by
> which the bequest of his
> said ..."

And,

> "... 'one negro boy
> Jesse $651'; sold for
> $450, one negro boy Nathan
> $621'; sold for $450, one
> negro girl Mariah $300';
> sold for $300" (Slave
> Information from Various

Loudoun Co., VA Documents,
pages 6 and 12)

Apparently, the slave masters had full control to operate with impunity among the slaves. As the result, the selling of other human beings continued unabated for two decades.

The results were devastating to the families. Mothers were in most cases permanently separated from their children or "husbands." Husbands were separated from their wives, brothers from sisters, other family members from other family members. These effects were traumatic and long lasting to those slaves who had to experience this cruelty. Today, most African-Americans can only trace family relatives up until a certain time or place. Due to the horrors of slavery, much of the history of the descendants for African-Americans is lost forever.

Some Realities of Slavery; Lack of Education for Slaves

Another law of slavery that did not affect Mammy Judy's circumstances was the prohibition against teaching slaves to read. Elizabeth Grinton states in the *Treasure Troves* introduction that Ms. Mamie Barber, the master's daughter, taught Mammy Judy how to read. But according to a passage from a classroom handout Excerpts from U.S. Slave Excerpts, a North Carolinian law stated,

> Any free person who
> shall hereafter teach, or
> attempt to teach, any
> slave within this state to
> read or write, the use of
> figures excepted, or shall
> give or sell to such slave
> or slaves any books or
> pamphlets, shall be liable
> to indictment … and upon
> conviction shall, at the
> discretion of the court,
> if a white man or woman,
> be fined not less than one
> hundred dollars, nor more
> than two hundred dollars,
> or imprisoned; and if a
> free person of colour,
> shall be fined, imprisoned
> or whipped, at the
> discretion of the court,
> not exceeding thirty-nine
> lashes, nor less than
> twenty lashes … And for a
> similar offense as to
> instruction, a slave shall
> receive thirty-nine lashes
> on his or her bare back.
> (North Carolina)

Consequently, Mamie Barber could have been indicted and charged in regard to teaching Mammy Judy to read. But according to comments in an article from the *Britannica Online* title Black Code, such restrictions were not always enforced.

"Slave codes were not always strictly enforced, but whenever any signs of unrest were detected the appropriate machinery of the state would be alerted and the laws more strictly enforced." (Britannica Online, p. 1)

Many of the descendants of Mammy Judy became successful in their own personal lives, becoming public workers, teachers, and performers in the arts.

Analysis of Elizabeth Grinton's Treasure Troves

In the introduction to *Treasure Troves*, The Life of Judith Barber (Grand Mammy Judy, 1820-1912), Mrs. Grinton's style of writing seems constrained. This style is similar to the slave narratives of Phyllis Wheatley. Both authors attempt to accommodate their readers, leaving out offensive or stark words that would shock the senses rather than placate. For example, in writing to the Earl of Dartmouth, William Legge, Wheatley's passionate plea for freedom for her fellow slaves relied on eliciting compassion to achieve a favorable response from Lord Dartmouth. She writes in stanza number 20,

Should you, my lord, while you peruse my song,

Wonder from whence my love of Freedom sprung,

Whence flow these wishes for the common good,

By feeling hearts alone best understood,

I, young in life, by seeming cruel fate

Was shatch'd from *Afric's* fancy'd happy seat;

What pangs excruciating must molest,

What sorrows labour in my parent's breast?

Steel'd was that soul and by no misery belov'd:

Such, such my case. And can I then but pray

Others may never feel tyrannic sway?

In comparing Wheatley's calm approach to the direct, blunt approach used by Frederick Douglass in his *Narratives of the Life of Frederick Douglass*, one can see the contrast in styles. Douglass quotes Mr. Auld, who had just ordered Mrs. Auld not to teach him (Douglass) to read,

> To use his own words, further, he said, 'If you give a nigger an inch, he will take an ell. A nigger should know nothing but to obey his master—to do as he is told to do. Learning would spoil the best

nigger in the world.
'Now,' said he, 'if you
teach that nigger
(speaking of myself) how
to read, there would be no
keeping him.' (*The Norton
Anthology of African
American Literature*, p.
325)

Elizabeth Grinton's approach is similarly indirect to Wheatley's in relating the story of Mammy Judy in *Treasure Troves* based on the textural examples available. Her introduction, titled *The Life of Judith Barber*, Grinton does not give many details of the cruel aspects of Mammy Judy life on the plantation, nor does the article written in the *Genealogy of Wilkes County* recount any hardships. Particular attention is given by Grinton in the article to tactfully stress the cooperation of current family members of the Barber family in "providing information" for the article. Nor did Mrs. Grinton address the cruelty of slavery when she talked of Mammy Judy's "job assignments." "Job" as in being paid for services. To be clear, Mammy Judy was never paid for her work as a slave. Her chores were passed down to her children as she grew too old to complete them. Such was the custom of the cruel system of slavery.

Free at Last ...

Emancipation for slaves in North Carolina came in 1865 (two years after President

Lincoln issued the proclamation), when General Joseph Johnston surrendered the last confederate soldiers to General William Sherman on April 26, 1865. The state of North Carolina was readmitted to the union in 1868, and slavery was deemed illegal. The United States congress also passed the 14th amendment in 1868, granting blacks equal citizenship and civil rights. A Civil Rights bill was also passed in congress in 1875, giving blacks equal treatment and other rights of citizens. But the legacy of slavery still haunted Mammy Judy and other former slaves in that region. The Grandfather Clause, which only gave freedom to slaves if their grandfather had been free during a certain time period, was created to frustrate new laws regarding slavery. The *Slave Codes*, which ruled every aspect of their life, were replaced after emancipation by the *Black Codes*. These codes also were developed to impede the progress toward freedom for the Negroes. In spite of these attempts to subvert justice, former slaves persevered, and fought these injustices created by those who refused to give up the life of ease which they felt that they deserved as the "superior" race.

Eventually, Mammy Judy did obtain her freedom from the Barber family. Elizabeth Barber relates how Annie, who had found and returned the body (or bodies) of Alice and Martha, also requested that the Barber family release Mammy Judy into her care. The Barber family refused, even though slavery was now clearly illegal. Annie persisted in her request for Mammy Judy removal into her care.

Although the Barbers considered taking Annie to court, they finally relented, and allowed Mammy Judy to move away. Mammy Judy lived with Annie until her death on September 8, 1912. According to a personal account by Elizabeth Grinton, Annie made Mammy Judy a dress, just to wear around the house. But Mammy Judy loved the dress so much that she requested to be buried wearing it. Her request was complied with by the current descendants of the former slave now known as Aunt Judy.

Now we have Mama's brothers and sisters to thank for carrying on their legacy, starting from Grandpa Burl and Mommy, including Uncle "Urban" Ervin, who retired from being a bishop at Shiloh Baptist Church in Ohio. And the other living sister is Linda Millsap Jones. She too is an Apostle, and has a doctorate. Her church name is R.O.M.A. Unfortunately, her husband, and our cousin Bill Jones, who was the senior co-pastor, passed away.

Mama also had other brothers. Their names are Jeremiah, Ezra, Wallace, Curlee, Luke. She also had a sister named Estelle. The four brothers have passed on to God's Kingdom. Mama's father was Rev. Anthony Burley Millsap. His first wife passed away. His second wife was Alma. Mama and she talked daily. When Alma, aka "Mommie," would call, I would say, "Mama, Mommie is on the phone!" I love my Mama's family. When we were kids, Mama and Daddy would drive us to Grandpa and Grandma's house. On occasion, our parents let us stay overnight. But on those short visits, Grandpa would pull out a candy cane. A thick one too. I would sit behind Grandpa and rub his head. He would fall asleep. He was bald. He would wake up but would go back. Mary and Linda were close in age. So those two hung out together a lot. After a while, Linda moved away. As did Mary, to college. The two of them are still very close and do talk often on the phone. Linda is in Ohio, and Mary in California. The picture is of Mama and her sister, Dr. Linda Jones. Below are Pastor Linda, Bishop E. Ervin Millsap, and Curley Millsap, all Mama's brothers.

Senior Pastor Glenn William Jones and his wife, Dr. Linda Millsap Jones

The two prophetic dreams of Mama's passing

Chapter 14:
Mama, the Lord shows His seers in advance

One thing that always impressed me about our parents was their joy of praying. I found out later in life that Mom Bessie, Daddy's Mama, was a prayer intercessor. Again, Daddy and Mama had us children on our knees praying a few times, as Reverend Moore had issued a challenge to our church to take a few nights to pray with your family, which was good. However, Daddy decided to do it on a weeknight, while our television programs were on. After a couple of nights of that, one of the siblings must have talked to Mama. So, the experiment stopped. But as you can see, this episode made an impression on me, even to this day. I am not an intercessor, but I have been part of teams at the few churches I attended. I learned to pray in intimate settings with Jesus. This grew into something I never expected or even thought could happen. He spoke back! Jesus talks a lot, once He has established that intimacy with you in your special setting. One of the special developments was how God taught me to journal, and write down what He told me to write. I wanted to share with you one of these encounters.

As God has revealed to me that I have a gift as a prophet and a seer of dreams. So, I think it good here at this time to include circumstances of dreams that occurred concerning my Mama's death. For some of my siblings, this will be the first time that they've heard about the dreams.

These dreams came at a time when I was attempting to learn how to interpret dreams. I loved watching the Prophet and teacher John Paul Jackson, where he taught how to interpret dreams. I watched for years. I even purchased his and other well-known dream interpreters' books. I had really gotten good at it. I still had to look at some books to find the meaning of objects, or colors, or animals. I learned the difference between a dream that had a lot of symbolism and prophetic information. I knew the difference of what each was. This night, it was prophetic, and needed little interpretation.

The first dream began with my standing in a dimly lit room. In front of me was my main angel, Weapon. Usually when I saw Weapon in a dream, he had a big smile. For the first time, he was not smiling. In fact, he was somber. He looked at me, and directed my gaze toward the room we were standing in. In front of me, I could see furniture. A couch and a single chair. Beyond the couch were shelves, as they were also to my left behind Weapon. On the shelves were different suitcases, all different sizes. One was a small handbag, the other a carry-on. They were all the same color. Black. In front of me, I saw a shelf with creamy white pearls laying on them. They were long and were seashells. Then I saw a suitcase that looked like one I had, with dark green flowers and a background of hunter green. I picked it up and wondered why that was the only one suitcase that had any color. To the next scene.

I was standing outside a building. It was a train terminal, and it was daylight. I stood in front of the tracks. Beside me was what I thought was cement sitting blocks. They were oddly shaped, longer than most sitting blocks, and there was only three. One was low; the next attached was higher; the center was the tallest. Also standing at these blocks was a man. He stared out into the distance. He was clammy and pale, and you could see the veins under his face's skin. He kept staring away into the distance. I tried to talk with him to say hello. I asked him his name. He ignored me. Then I looked to my right. There was a train, modern, and its door was open. I saw a red purse sitting in an empty chair. I also saw the back of one of my older friends whom I hadn't seen in a while. She had been seriously ill. Her back was to me as I looked at her from the back. She had on a black dress, and she was looking out the window of the train. She was leaning into it, with a forlorn look. She appeared to be expecting someone, and she seemed to be impatient.

I looked to the back of the train. There I saw my Mama. She too was in a black dress. I wondered why she was sitting in the back of the train, and not even in a seat. She was sitting on a riser, with a bucket for a seat underneath her. She also had three suitcases, all black too. They were the same size. She balanced them with her hands. She had a large smile on her face as she looked at me. But why there? I tried to get on the modern train, but it moved away from the curve. I wanted to get on the train because I wanted to be with my Mama. And every time I attempted to get on, strangely the train appeared to avoid my every move. Then the doors closed. After that, the train tracks disappeared. The road suddenly changed into a street. I could see a city to my left. I was standing on a hill, looking down at it. A large city. Then all of a sudden, water came rushing down the street. Muddy water. It covered the street and floated the train. I looked back at the cement pillars, and the pale man was gone. The dream ended.

A couple of years later, I had another dream. As this dream began, I "awakened" or saw myself in my house. I stood in the hallway of our home in North Carolina. This hallway held my parents' clothing. The lighting was dim. In the next scene, I stood in the entry to the den from the bottom of the stairwell. I watched as my father, dressed in a black Army dress uniform, held the reins of a black horse in full regalia. He led the horse in a completed circle with the bridle. I thought the horse was like the one that was in President Kennedy's funeral, Black Jack. In this scene, the horse that

Father led had the boots pointed backyard as well, signifying the death of the owner.

In the next scene, the horse had disappeared. My father stood there in the middle of the room. Then he began to turn in a circle with his arm outstretched to complete it. I heard a voice say, "Gather the family." Then all my brothers and sisters, with much somberness, appeared in the room. They all clasped hands to make a circle after as he waited and stood there with Father. He still wore the formal Army military uniform that the soldier did in President John Kennedy's funeral. I didn't get into or join the circle. I didn't want to. I felt the sadness and heavy gloom in the room. The high honor of someone who was revered had died. In the nation's mourning of President Kennedy's assassination, those feelings too were being felt within homes and on the Washington streets. A very sad spectacle. The dream ended.

At the time of my mother's death three years later, the Lord God revealed the meaning of both these dreams. I'm glad He waited, because I would not have been able to stand knowing before she passed.

The first dream about the train changed from sitting on a train track to a floating landing craft air-cushion boat. It floated away from me when I tried to board it. I wanted to be with my mother. The reason: it was telling me that her death would be coming up.

When I saw my angel, Weapon, it was in an environment that he had never appeared before me. Weapon always smiled when I saw him in my prophetic dreams. He wore regular clothing and never blinked. But in this dream, the environment was gloomy and sad. Weapon did not smile. I asked him why. He didn't speak back this time either. He pointed to the shelves that held all types of suitcases in various sizes. He motioned for me to check them out with his hand. As I said before, I walked up to inspect the suitcases. What God revealed to me at this point was there were different suitcases, but one was different. All the other suitcases were black. That meant that these waited for other people when it would be time for them to die. But the one overnight bag I picked up resembled my own overnight suitcase, with the same colors. Very different from the black ones. Also, I was a string of pearls on the shelf. I love pearls, as did Mama. Remember they were seashells? I don't like seashell pearls, but my Sister Mom, Bettye, collected them.

The next scene of the cement sitting I saw, as God explained now to me, revealed they were actually mausoleums: three of them stacked together, indicating different heights. The first one was lower, the second one higher, the third at the same lower height of the first. The Lord God continued.

The man I saw, whom I thought was an engineer or worker for the railroad, was actually "Death." The Lord pointed out that the death angel was pale and appeared clammy. The Lord God then told me that when I saw Barbara, my friend sitting on the train with her back to me, she was impatiently waiting for me (Him). She was looking for me to come and take her out of this world. She was ready to go home to Heaven. The Lord God then explained that the only reason he could get my attention to look at a different subject was by using a red purse. This why God had sat the purse in the first seat in front of me. And I saw it as I looked inside the train. I noted that God that had always used a red purse in some of my dream. And has always been the case between Him and me in other prophetic dreams.

The Lord God continued. "You noted that you turned and saw your mother sitting on a small stool trying to keep her balance on it, almost falling off." I said yes. He continued. "She had three suitcases in her hands: small, medium, and large. Just like the heights of the mausoleum." I said yes. The Lord God said the suitcases refer to the years she had left on this earth, which was three. The short stool meant that her time was "short" on this earth. And He continued, "You noted she was happy and not ill. But ready to go." I said yes to Him. I can say here that when Mama did die it was not from disease, but natural causes.

The Lord God continued. "You wanted to get on the train, in the seat where your red purse sat." I said yes. God said, "But when you tried to get on the train to sit with your mother, the door closed. The train turned from a rail express to a floating train with an amphibious rake." I said yes. The Lord God said, "You still fought to get on the train, now train-boat, and it floated away." Yes, I said. "You also saw then as you turned to ask the porter for help, that he had disappeared." Yes, I said. "Looking toward the city down the hill, the train/amphibious transportation moved away from you." Yes, Lord. "That meant that it wasn't your time to go home to Heaven. That is why your suitcase appeared as normal to you. Your turn had not come to die. Unlike your mother and friend Barbara. Their times were coming due to passing over to me." He said that Barbara was sitting in the "first seat" directly in front of my seat, facing front. Her back was turned to me and I couldn't see her face. That meant she had one more year on earth. The Lord God continued, "The city you saw represented the City of God. My city." I, Bessie, believe that was where the train/landing craft went.

From the date of this first dream to this revelation from God, my mother's death was three years away. In addition, Barbara, my friend, died a year later after this dream. In fact, I went to her funeral. I signed the book of visitors. The Lord prompted me to go over and view the table that had Barbara's memories and pictures. Her husband had been her constant companion and caregiver for years as Barbara's health declined. He was always joyful and never complained. He didn't get a lot of sleep because Barbara's needs were constant. Whenever I saw Orlie and Barbra at events before this when she couldn't travel, he was loving and kind as usual. Their example to me was how a marriage should be. Until death do us part.

However, as, I viewed the articles on the table, I stood back, stunned. On the table lay a long string of "seashell pearls." The same pearls that God had shown me in my prophetic dream—the identical pearls I handled on the shelf that the angel, Weapon, pointed out to me. And it had been a year from the date of the dream. I was in shock, even though I had been told about them by the Lord God.

The prophetic dreams interpreted to me by the Lord God are some of the most important ones I hold dear. Mainly because they concerned persons I love: my mother and friend Barbara. Hopefully you can pray about how God can talk to you on a personal level. His plan for you will be totally different from mine. Let Him speak to you about the destiny He has for you. He waits for you too.

Chapter 15:
Daddy's lineage and Macedonia Baptist Church

Uncle Harve with sisters Aunt East and Katherine

My father initially was a farmer. His family owned fourteen acres. His father, unknown to me, was someone who reared him and his brothers; and I'm not sure why. They had the name of Stokes, but that changed to the man that Mama said "raised them," which was Mayes. And he was Caucasian.

My father and his father, Gabriel (Gabe), along with (Mom) Bessie, were the ones who started the church. "Mom Bessie" was born May 1, 1882, and died on January 31, 1950, of influenza and hypertension. Jack Crawford was her father, and Sarah Watts was her mother. Mom Bessie had other children besides my father. They were Jack, Louisa, and Katherine. Mom Bessie was known for being a prayer intercessor/warrior. There was one stepsister, Edna Crawford. Grandpa Gabe was born in 1891 and died in 1946. In fact, they actually built the first church. The building seated a little over two hundred. My father's dad, Gabe Mayes, was the founder of the church itself. I don't know the original size of the church that they built, but it stands today as a testament to those who would feel the love of Jesus to have a place of worship in a place for all to come.

According to Daddy, at one time the church caught on fire. Daddy told me that the wood-burning stove they used in those days caused the fire. They didn't have access to water, and I don't know if the fire department was called. But as the situation settled, Daddy and his father and brother Ted began to rebuild the church. They built it larger the second time around.

Macedonia Baptist Church, named by my father and his brothers in 1860, was a part of a community of people who worked hard and reared children who gave love for others and helped anyone for decades. There was an order of respect for elders during these times in our era, and a love of neighborhood and families. Some won't allow many in this nation now to even believe that this respect among people is still active. But it is, and actually has been growing because of the chaos and lies being fostered on our nation and others. My siblings were just as driven to show that respect to others around our town, and we all grew within their love for all people and nurtured those who needed it.

Daddy and Mama were a deacon and deaconess. Mama was the church's choir director and taught Sunday school. Our entire family at one time or another served in the choir. And Daddy was the steward who handled the money for the church. Mama used The Flower and Gift Shop on 1st S. Center Street run by "Miss" Elise for all the flowers displayed on the church pulpit and for funerals. I still use her to this day, as she is the best florist I know back there. She did the flowers for Macedonia and does Mama and Daddy's flowers for their grave on Mother's and Father's Day, and has done so unfortunately for other members of our family. Their stories to come.

My uncle Plez, Daddy's brother-in-law, was also a deacon as was his wife. His wife, Margaret (Aunt Mag), was our mom's best friend. They were like sisters, and talked for hours on the phone every day. And sometimes more than a few times, depending on news. Kay Ivey, my cousin, was Aunt Mag's daughter. Kay Baby had two daughters with her husband, Donald. They are Donna and Ashley. Both have gone on to make a home with their own families.

We spent weekends together. Our mom and dad, with us along, would go to Aunt Louise's (East) on some Sundays. That is where I learned about cows and milking them. Uncle Ed and Aunt Louise had a dairy farm. That is where we learned to how to make ice cream from a churn. I usually, as the youngest, had to turn the churn the most. But it was fun. Sometimes around sunset, the cows would go into the barn on their own to be milked by my cousins. I had noted earlier by the way that Mama and Aunt East must have been in competition for having babies. With every class, we had one cousin within it. So, the cousin of Uncle Ed and Aunt East was Charlie. He got tired of milking the cows, and just wanted to go off with friends.

Being somewhat curious, I went inside the barn and saw how they used automated pumps to extract the milk and washed any cow "pods" away with a hose, keeping the product area clean. Oh man did it smell!!!!

Now when it was Uncle Plez and Aunt Mag's turn, we would play outside with Kay. We were fascinated by Kay's new playhouse. Uncle Plez had built it especially for her. His lawns were manicured and the space was large. A grove of trees lined the side, a far distance away. He had white picket fences that surrounded his house. On occasion, we would run into the Jones there. We just all sat around and watched television. I loved those days. And yes, we are all still close.

Aunt Katheryn ("Kat") was Daddy's other sister. Aunt Kat lived in Washington, DC, so we didn't see her and her husband but once every two years, if that. She was stylish, and spoke not with a southern accent but a northern accent. After her husband died decades later, Aunt Kat decided to get a part-time job just to have something to do, as a school bus driver. She became even more well known in the community than she had before. Aunt Kat also took her church responsibilities just as seriously, working with different organizations and serving in any capacity that needed her help.

Aunt East, on the other hand, was a stay-at-home mom. She took care of my cousins, which was tough. There was Glenn, Waitsal, George, Donnie, Charlie, and Macy. Macy is a reverend now, preaching around the nation. She also preaches at Macedonia Baptist Church on many occasions. Of the family, Martha Jane, Lorette (and husband Johnathan), Brenda, and (Reverend) Macy are alive. Uncle Woodrow Millsap's house was fun to visit too. Woodrow was the church director of music for a time. Ruth Millsape was a professional seamstress. She was so calming to be around, and talked while she worked at her sewing machine. She would have cut fabric all around her. Their children were Cheryl and Meryl. We still stay in touch over the years.

As I grew up in Macedonia, having a dad and mom who were officials in the church got you many things. And you also had to put out more effort than others because of that role of parents. But there was fun stuff. One was when the Deacon Board would scout places for our annual church picnic. Now the Deacon Board had Mama and Daddy as I said before. But it also had Uncle Plez (Mag), (Uncle) Rock, (Aunt) Georgia, and Eli Hill Sr. We all jumped in our cars and caravanned into the mountains to inspect those sites that would be ideal for the entire church to picnic. We had so much fun.

Chapter 16:
All about Bettye and Russell; and the Lackeys

My "sister mom" Bettye and her husband Russell, daughter Sonya, and their grandchildren Kenadra and Nicholas

From the eldest to the youngest, and after the first babies born:

My sister Bettye had always been the next in charge, or the final decision-maker in our family. As the eldest, she reported to our parents, who relied on her for counsel in all areas of life. Bettye has a master's degree in education and was a teacher at Unity High School for decades. She was a wise and sensitive woman. I knew her to be kind, caring, and one who took personal interest in my well-being. She was always there for me to talk to. She was the one whom I looked to as being a semi-parent, even though a sibling. I went to Mama and Daddy for answers, and I went to her too to see where she stood. And whether I agree with her counsel or not, she never once blocked me from her opinions.

For a while, she and I looked at life differently as I grew up. She, a married woman with family responsibilities, was more mature. I, as a single woman, couldn't relate. I do remember with great heartbreak one thing that placed her in my high esteem. After she had her first child, Sonya Lackey, she and Russell decided that in order to keep working and have income for her family, a full daycare provider would be needed. I don't know the circumstances as to how the decision was made, but she arranged with Mama and Daddy to keep her two-year-old first daughter Sonya at our house in Taylorsville. What a noble concept, and a painful one for her and Russell to handle. She and Russell would come up to our house and take her home on weekends. But on weekdays, Sonya stayed with Mama and Daddy. After about a year, emotionally, the arrangement wasn't working for either of them. Mama and Daddy concurred. As our parents, they knew the importance of bonding with the child in the first formative years.

So, Bettye and Russell decided to make other arrangements with people in their neighborhoods to take care of Sonya while she and Russell worked. I can remember vividly the times Bettye wept, vigorously saying goodbye to her daughter on Sunday nights. Mama would take Sonya into her and Daddy's bedroom so Sonya wouldn't see Bettye crying as she left out the back door of the kitchen. So, all that ended, and there were no repercussions from the arrangement. But for me, the departure scenes were heartbreak, seeing her leaving her baby in Taylorsville.

While Sonya was living with us during that short period of time, she and Nana and "Harvey," as she called them, experienced the fun of Daddy taking her for rides or allowing her to tag along on other outings. She learned all the routes to and fro, and could tell anyone where to go.

I also remember when I spent time with Bettye visiting on weekends. Bettye told me that Sonya could tell me where to turn and what route to take to downtown Statesville. Sonya would perch on the armrest in the front seat of the car. And true to Bettye's instructions, Sonya directed me to the bank the parents used so I could deposit money, and then home again. Sonya has always had a high IQ. Sonya's grammar school bored Sonya, and Bettye and Russell had to make a decision to place her in the next grade up, or leave her bored but with her age group. I voted for moving her to a higher grade, skipping one, but her parents decided to keep her where she was with her age group to allow her to remain with an age group she could understand. Thus, the first grandchild of Harve and Lucille Mayes was returned to her home in Statesville permanently.

The Lord told me in June 2018 that Bettye, due to health issues, would soon pass away. I did thank God for this information, as He did it as He talked to me in my journal. The Lord told me, "That's when I began to call her on a more daily basis." Later, the Lord God told me that Bettye was made aware of why I "was calling her so much." So, she knew that I knew. It didn't matter. I was about to lose my "sister mom," which was just as devastating to me as losing my own mother again. Bettye took the calls from me without any reservations. She talked as much as she could, as the disease had begun to take a more dominant toll on her breathing. I cried; I was inconsolable. I cried the same way after the viewing of her body outside church that night. I still don't know why. But that I would *never* be able to see and talk to a person who, in so much of my growing up and as an adult on my own, was no more on earth. I still am in a way emotional about Bettye's life on earth. At her funeral, arranged by her immediate family, I saw how Bettye's life affected so many around the state and the nation.

I had no idea, until the funeral. I had met Sister Mom's director of the AME Zion association. But at the funeral, I heard him speak. The man who sits on President Trump's religious board. He did the eulogy. The funeral had to be held at a larger church, which Sonya found, due to her mother's impact on so many people. Her funeral had an escort too. I was amazed how long the procession was. When we as a family arrived at her funeral, I saw thousands already there and more coming inside. Bettye's bishop was the host, one of Sister Mom's protégés, and other officials and entire organizations from around the nation were there. Again, I learned of how wide her reach was in the Lord God's Kingdom, and saw how many people she had influenced with her example and prayer.

Sister Mom had many, as she called, daughters in the Lord. Sonya, her dad Russell, Bettye's husband, and Rusty her brother worked hard and had to postpone their grief for four days. In fact, buses of people came to the Shiloh Church for the wake because no building could hold what the family knew would be massive overflow of mourners to come.

A story about Rusty, Bettye's son: On a rainy night, while emptying the trash, we heard a cry of "meow." Rusty went in the rain to investigate. He followed the sound, and discovered a little kitten. He picked the tiny kitten up and said, "Poor little kitten. I lost my Mama too." Rusty then took the kitten into his parents' house, where he was staying with his dad, Russell. NO animal had EVER been in that house. BUT! Rusty kept him there for a time. He told Sonya about the kitten, and she was shocked to know that their dad had allowed the kitten to stay there. In fact, we were sent pictures with what Rusty named "Sue," Bettye's middle name. We all thought the tiny kitten was a girl. Later they found out, as the kitten grew up, that she was in fact a he! I suggested that they keep the name Sue, and use the Japanese version for a reason in case anyone asked. Rusty now has two cats, as he also found another kitten.

By the way, as Sonya was doing the eulogy for the family, she mentioned the kitten; that got a little laugh from the family. It was an inside joke. Mary and I, who were seated in the second row, poked Rusty from behind. He had laughed too when Sonya called the name, "Six Weeks." A name she called the first kitten. Sonya said also that "2.0 was her, but 3.0 was Kenadra." Rusty's daughter had taken on the legacy as well of their mom, who was 1.0. Kendra helped her grandmother and grandfather on a weekly basis with tasks related to Shiloh. She put together a program of what Sister Mom told her every Sunday. She helped Sister Mom Bettye, and Russell Big Bro (to me), all the time, even when she went off to college.

Her dad Rusty and mom Nicole had another child named Nicholas. He has preached his first sermon, and is still deeply involved in the tasks that God assigns him to do as a possible minister of the gospel. Again, Mama and Daddy's legacy continues on through the siblings and the grandchildren, and keeps on to this day. It's a legacy of a loving God and His path, caring and loving others no matter their circumstances, and showing the love of God to countless people around the Republic. The Lord God Jesus has triumphed in the known and in many cases the unknown avenues. Yes, even to the great-grands, who Mama and Daddy got to see. One family being Jim, or James Sr. And we began on him, number seven of those who survived of the eleven that Mama and Daddy had.

Bettye and Russell had to give speeches to the organizations they led around the nations. In those speeches were scriptures of God's love, and they inspired the audience to come to Jesus as their personal Savior. Nicholas saw this growing up. Thus, he decided to do the same thing after receiving the Lord God in his heart. Sonya, at her church, has also given messages. She is the head of the hospitality group, which sets up and manages the daily working of events or repass for the church. She was the one who was first of the siblings in their family to give public addresses. Her tasks are many, and her actions help the church events that bring in thousands for annual church meetings from around the nation. Sonya has two master's degrees, and works the state of North Carolina as a manager. Rusty works for Home Depot as team lead. That's why I say known and unknown, as even their own legacy in God continues to this day.

Bettye's (Sister Mom's) and Lackey family

Mt. Zion Baptist Church was built by the Lackey family. Much like our dad and his family, the Lackeys also had a Lackey compound where the children had their own property. The heads of theirs were Bettye's father and mother-in-law, Mrs. Effie and Mr. Joe Lackey.

Mr. Joe and his wife, Mrs. Effie, were the pioneers for their family. In fact, my older sister Bettye married into the Lackey family and to Russell. A man I consider my other big brother. Russell had four brothers and three sisters. Their family began a church too, much as our parents did, called Mount Zion Baptist Church. To this day, both churches stand as a monument of love for Jesus Christ, and Almighty God and the Holy Spirit, and welcome all who come to its doors. "Mr. Joe" was a farmer with large acreages of land. He farmed the land and profited from the produce he grew every year. He grew corn with stalks so big and tall that you couldn't see over the top of them. The crop went for miles. He planted and grew other produce. All was harvested by his sons and friends.

After Bettye married Russell, I remember where even the Mayes family helped in putting their family harvest away. Mrs. Effie canned the corn and other products like tomatoes. The work was in her kitchen in their very large home. And just like our Mama when cooking and canning produce, an assembly line was formed. As families, the older sibling women helped her cook some of the soup she'd made from the corn and tomatoes into jars. Outside, the boys helped with picking the corn and shucking the ears of corn for the soup and dry storage. The Lackeys, to this day, helped their community grow and thrive, as did the Mayes.

Bettye and Russell went on to prosperous careers. To this day, Sonya is still the genius she has always been. She owns her home in Greensboro. She graduated as an accountant from college. She now has two master's in business relations. Rusty, her little brother, has had a successful career in retail too. He grows vegetables in the summer behind his and Nicole's ranch-style home, and has become known as the best barbecue in the family. He has been the backbone of Shiloh Church. His son Nicholas preached one of his first sermons there, and all the family is very proud of the role in ministry he has chosen.

Bettye has followed in our parents' footsteps, caring for others and educating people as a leader of various departments in the African Methodist Episcopal Zion Church (AME) organization. Earlier in her adulthood, she graduated at the top of her class as valedictorian from Livingstone College with honors in 1960. Her education was funded at first by Mr. Hinshaw. Then the funding was taken over by Daddy and Mama.

Here is a part of biography from Sonya, her daughter, about her life:

> Bettye's first and only job was at Wayside School. She retired in 1995 as a classroom teacher for thirty-four plus years. She was named teacher of the year at Wayside school at least five times starting in 1969. In 1987, she was presented the Long Leaf Pine Certificate by Governor James Martin for her volunteer services with the Statesville Chamber of Commerce's Education Committee. Her Master's degree project was published in the National Education Journal in 1990. Through her labor of love, she touched the lives of many through her love for God's people. At Macedonia Baptist Church, her former church, she was a member of the choir, usher board, and Sunday School and Christian Education Directory. At Shiloh, she was a Sunday School Teacher, a member of the Deaconess Board, User Board, Christian Ed. Dept., Parent Body, Stewardess Board., Life member of the Missionary Society, Trustee Board as Chairman 1995-1999, Chancel Choir, Building Committee, and Lay Council. In external organizations, Bettye worked as a member at the conference level of these same organizations which included the

Camp Dorothy Walls, a member of the Albert South Scholarship Fund, Vice Chair of the Yokefellow Ministries and on its Board of Directors, assisted at Fifth Street Ministries during the Thanksgiving and Christmas seasons, and was on the Chamber of Commerce Education Committee. Likewise, Russell and she partnered with other organizations, some of which he led which includes Director of Ushers at the local, state, and national levels.

Again, Bettye was the acknowledged head of our family after Mama and Daddy passed away. Until reading her biography from the funeral (above), some of us didn't realize how ensconced she was in her church community, always putting others first. Mary and I didn't know the amount or depth of her caring, because she never talked to us about it. She was humble. We knew, and chided her for doing too much. But she was always volunteering to do the heavy work and be the leader in her expertise in education and organization skills, without complaint. In fact, she loved doing these projects. And also tackled issues within their church association on a national basis. She and Russell Lackey, her husband, flew to conferences as leads of large organizations in the Methodist church. Both of them were leaders of national and international organizations under AME Zion Shiloh church. There were many honors they received both in and out of this association. Honors seemed to grow on the walls of their homes, just like Mama and Daddy had awards hanging on their walls for various accomplishments in their community.

I adored Bettye. We all did. She was my example in many ways. I know my brothers and sister believe and felt that about her too. We took her passing hard, especially Junior. She lived there in North

Carolina in a town nearby. So, Junior and the others got to interact with her more often than Mary, Thomas, and me, who live in California. I know they were devastated, even though it was inevitable. But Mary and I were just as devastated, as she was ours and their "sister mom." She called every weekend, as I said before. And rare was the Sunday call missed by any of us in the family. No one existed like her. No one.

I knew that my sister's health was failing. To comfort me, the Lord spoke to me in detail, to help me cope when it happened. Below is what God spoke to me on her passing, sometimes months in advance. Sonya and I spoke about these revelations on the phone, and others. I believe that by doing so, it helped her and others to understand and absorb her ordeal.

I sent this vision and revelation from God to the Lackey family sometime after the funeral. It's here verbatim with their permission:

May 5, 2018

I have seen parts of Jesus (this moment today), but now I see most of His body. First the hand of God to the right hand of fellowship. Then the arm, then your entire face to your waist. But who is the man I see in the suit?

(God speaks to me) "It's your father. Look at his face again, then decide. Slow down, learn, look and listen. You don't always know where I AM going or where I AM about to do. What I am about to do is take your Bettye home. Your Daddy will meet her and carry her on to Glory. A Glory she deserves for her house and for other people in the community. Mrs. Lackey and Russell see the changes in her demeanor and saw the changes in her body. He wanted her to go on and live with him on earth. But she is ready to go home with Jesus. She is tired. Your sister is tired of this earth and this land. Mama and Daddy will escort her. Do not call her back to you. She wants to go.

That is the answer, baby sister. She is ready to go. She is ready to go right now, baby sister, and rest in her Kingdom too. You'll be lonely without her being around. But take care. I will take care of her needs in Heaven and love her like I would have done. Take care, Daughter, and let her go. I'll send someone to help you and Mary and Thomas with the means. Stop regretting her loss. She will be with me ... Comfort my friend. Lucille will meet her daughter and praise her for her good deeds at home and abroad for the Kingdom. For my Kingdom. She has fought the battle and she, Bettye, has won. She will do well, glorious, in Heaven as a witness. My witness for my Kingdom to come on Earth as it is in Heaven. She will be relieved of duties. Her duties that she carried out in my Kingdom for my Glory."

I see (vision) an opening of a casket in a grand opulent place like where Barbara Bush was honored. Then I heard these words:

"It's going to get worse, Bee. She won't be able to breath after a while. She will wonder what's going on. (Heard Sonya say, "My Mama is going to die" in a matter-of-fact tone). She can hardly breathe now. She has had to slow down so much now. Now she knows there is no cure for her, and so she is ready to go home soon... She has made up her mind that she is going home. She is staying home to last as long as she can. But again, she no longer can breathe. She throws her food as she lives day by day. It hurts her to eat and breathe in. To inhale food down her throat just like your Daddy did in the hospital. So, let her go. She'll be okay for the journey. She wants to be with her daddy and Mama, Paw Paw. Just let her go. She is going to go anyway. Let her go. And Russell won't struggle. He will survive as I told you he would. But! He will miss her just like Sonya. Sonya will miss joking around with her and calling her Mama. Mama for such a long time.... We've been in this for a long time. Bettye and I. Russell will not like it. But Bettye needs to come home now while she can still breathe clearly. She is my Daughter and Russell is my son ... Sonya will stand tall like Sonya always has done as she learned it from me.... Tell them this for me. Tell them this is for their Mama. Bettye needs to be in the hospital under anesthesia. You understand? Her days won't be long and she won't stay on earth because she is tired. Tired of the strain of it all. The strain on her body, her lungs, her whole body. Her whole being... She needs to be in the hospital right now. But she won't survive there. She is already on her way home here to be with me and your daddy. Bettye and Russell will leave a legacy our family. Russell's family too. This will be the example needed for the entire nation. She needs to retire from the things of this world and reside in Heaven. She has done her tasks well. Very well. She'll be considered a champion when she arrives here. For me, it was a good death without problems or any assistance. Bettye may experience some problems, but she will get through them all without failure of any kind. She is and has always will be forever and eternity.... Take her to the hospital in August. That will be the time when Bettye will fail. And then my Bettye will come up and live and her Daddy Harve again. Russell should start taking care of her business. I talked to him about that, and he told me that he would begin that....

(ME: Song "Hills and Valleys" in my ear. Bettye is in the hospital tonight (8/19/18). Sonya told Russell to take all his meds that he would take in the mornings. Sonya sounded worried this time although she attempted humor to laugh this off. Sonya and Rusty are worried and sense this is not the norm for a visit to emergency for Bettye. Maybe I am reading too much into it. But given what you told me; this is it. But thy will be done.)

(H) "Bettye, she's hanging in there as best as she could. Please comfort Bettye and Russell and all friends around the world this night."

June 26, 2018

"Love your sister Bettye because she will die soon and Russell will be mad for a time, but not at you or Mary because you all loved her just as much as she cared for you and all of us."

August 5, 2018

"She doesn't know it yet, but she will do good here in Heaven despite her hopes to stay on earth and finish her job. She will do well here and she will plan and grow up here. She won't be asleep and will help you and Mary when she gets here to stay the course on earth as it is in Heaven. And Russell will have no other choice but to deal with Bettye's death."

August 19, 2018-September 19, 2018

From Bettye, last days.

"Tell Sonya I'll miss her. Tell Russell and Rusty I'll miss them too. Tell Russell and Rusty and Nicole that I love them. Tell Rusty and Nicole that I love them and not to let each other go. They'll understand. Bess, I am tired. I am tired of these struggles with this medicine and life has gone down the hill. My life is over on this earth. So, say farewell. Tell Buster that I love him. Jim also too and Pee-Wee and Junior. Also tell them not to cry. Tell Buster he is in charge of the family. He'll take issue with that. But then he'll take issue with anything. But now Bess, your sister is going to be fine. She is believing for my health. Now go home and go to sleep. I love you and take care of Sonya. She is having a hard time right now. Be at peace. Sonya won't cry. But she will when this is all over. Just like me and your daddy. He's here by the way and waiting on me like he uses to do with Carolyn. Mary. Tell her this is for me. She'll struggle too, but Buster will help her out...Take care. I've got to go. Your mother is here now and she is waiting for me. Tell them that Uncle Harve says hello. Tell Buster and Pee-Wee that they ought to know better than to cry like that. Don't cry like that again. Buster and Jim are torn up. But they'll survive. Now go home and sleep. I love you and take care of Sonya. She is having a hard time right now.

ME: Here is what I saw in a vision the time of Sis's transitioning.
**

Bettye said to me:

"Junior is coming off the truck. He'll be here soon." I saw Bettye in a dimly lit room. I saw Daddy and Mama standing there. They were wearing dark clothing. Then I saw Bettye. Her appearance had changed dramatically. Her clothing was dark, and her hair was very long and wavy. She had lost all the excess weight. She was in a perfect body. She was extremely animated in her new surroundings. She danced around as if she was not believing what she was seeing at that moment. She was very excited. Extremely excited. Very happy, running to and fro in multiple directions, laughing and saying, "I can't believe this!" She was breathing perfectly. No struggles as she breathed deeply without any effort or difficulty. She was exuberant, dancing around her environment. Then she suddenly disappeared from my sight. I wondered where she had gone, but Mama and Daddy were waiting patiently and looking at her with no stress. They were looking at the direction where she had gone. Then Bettye returned to Mama and Daddy in the room. What I described above was the conversation Bettye was having with me as she transitioned to the realm of Heaven. She went back, I believe, to make sure that she didn't do the final transition in front of Sonya who would soon leave for home. Both Sonya and I had this revelation, and she spoke it out to me as she drove home. She called and said, "okay. What did she say?" She meant Bettye talking to me. Rusty had called her back to the hospital to let her know that their mother had passed.

You called me, Sonya, and I explained to you what I just shared. How Bettye was very happy to be out of her body, even though that meant not being her dear family. Mama and Daddy did come to meet her and take her over to Heaven. But Bettye, being the wonderful person she was and is, wanted us here left on earth to know that she was happy. And although she was leaving our realm, she would still be looking out and praying for her family on earth. Bettye continued in the role of commander and said,

"Tell Mary I love her and to watch out for Jim, Junior, Pee-Wee, and Buster as they are having a hard time in particular. Be careful on the way home. Be safe. Buster and Jim are upset. Pee-Wee is crying. But Buster and Jim will be fine eventually. Junior won't be. In fact, he'll have a hard time. Then Buster will. Buster is on the phone right now. So, don't bother him right now. Junior will be back soon."

To me and them, Bettye said,

"Stop crying as this will upset people around you. Jim and Pee-Wee will be okay. Jim will cry but this is good for him. Be safe, ya'll hear?! Mama's here. All ya'll be safe you hear! Go home and be safe. Tickets for CA, we'll deal with it."

END

Addendum:

I know Sister Mom can breathe fully now, which is what we all wanted. You saw the worst of it when you were in her presence. But Bettye is fine now. And sometime in the future, we all will be too. None will ever forget. It's very hard.

Official Obituary for Bettye Sue (Mayes) Lackey

Mrs. Bettye Mayes Lackey, 79, of Statesville, peacefully transitioned on September 20, 2018 at Gordon Hospice House.

Mrs. Lackey was born in Alexander County, June 02, 1939, the daughter of the late Harvey Lee Mayes, Sr., and Lucille Elizabeth Millsaps Mayes. She was married to Russell Lackey for 58 years.

She graduated from Happy Plains High School in 1956 as valedictorian; Livingstone College in Salisbury, NC with honors in

1960; and with a M. Ed from UNC-Charlotte in 1990 as Suma cumin laude. She retired in 1995 as a classroom teacher for 34+ years. She was named teacher of the year at Wayside School at least five times, starting in 1969. In 1987, she was presented the Long Leaf Pine Certificate by Governor James Martin for her volunteer service with the Statesville Chamber of Commerce's Education Committee. Her Master's Degree project was published in the National Education Journal in 1990.

Mrs. Lackey touched the lives of many through her many labors of love. At Macedonia Baptist Church, her former church, she was a member of the choir, usher board, Sunday School, and Christian Education Director. At Shiloh, she was a Sunday School Teacher, a member of the Deaconess Board, Usher Board, Christian Ed. Dept., Parent Body, Stewardess Bd., Life Member of the Missionary Society, Trustee Board (Chairman 1995-1999), Chancel Choir, Building Committee, and Lay Council.

She served the Statesville District in some of the same organizations, having served as District Christian Education Director for twenty-four years. Bettye also worked with these organizations on the conference level and was a member of the Camp Dorothy Walls Trustee Board, vice chair of the Christian Education Board, DWCRC Mountaintop Gala, and a member of the Albert Stout Scholarship Fund. She was always willing to assist in many facets of the local, district, and conference church as needed.

For many years, Bettye's outreach included the community. She was vice chair of the Yokefellow Ministries and on its Board of Directors, assisted at Fifth Street Ministries during Thanksgiving and Christmas, and was on the Chamber of Commerce Education Committee.

Along with her beloved husband Russell, she is survived by one daughter, S. Lackey of Greensboro, NC, and one son, (Rusty) Jr. N.

Lackey, of Statesville; two grandchildren: K. Ai'Shai Lackey, and N. Lackey. She is also survived by a niece who was reared in the home, Mrs. C. Lackey Campbell of Casper, Ga., brothers, J. Mayes (Fleeta), H. Mayes (Linda), J. Mayes (Jean) and H. (Rhonda) Mayes Jr. and S. Primus, who was reared in the home, sisters M. Mayes and B. Mayes and M. Mayes and W. Howell who were reared in the home, one aunt, Pastor L. Millsaps Jones and one uncle, Bishop E. E. Millsaps, sisters-in-law, A. Rankin, L. Lackey, R. Lackey, A. Lackey, L. Lackey, J. Lackey and B. Lackey, brothers-in-law J. Lackey and H. T. Lackey, many church daughters and sons, cousins, nieces, nephews, friends, and the Shiloh Church Family.

END

Chapter 17:
Jessie (Buster) Mayes

Mama and Buster outside the house on a Sunday morning

Buster is the eldest sibling still alive. He and his wife Fleeta have been married for forty-five years. They have a son named Jessie Jr.

and a daughter named Monique Byers, my twin. Buster's nickname came about because of his love of boxing. His favorite boxer was Floyd Patterson. Buster is the sibling who had us boxing in the backyard. Once when my little brother Junior and I were having an argument, Buster made us put on his boxing gloves to resolve the issues. After a few hits and a little dancing around to avoid being hit, we became tired; Buster stopped us and declared both winners. Actually, Junior won the fight. I was too tired to do much more, and my anger was gone.

Buster also was the one for whom Daddy made the boxing room in the barn located in the back of our house. Nowadays, Buster has retired from his job at HT Hackney, but he still maintains a barbershop. He has a large client base. He told me how much he enjoys speaking with them, and giving advice. He has led quite a few to Lord Jesus. He has clients that are young and multi-generational. Buster is the third vice president of the NAACP in his region because of his outstanding work. Because of this, he was asked to be a delegate by the local Democratic Party, and also received a D.A.D. award for being a local Democrat supporter.

Buster is now the chairman of the Deacon Board and trustee at Macedonia Church, and he visits those members in the hospitals every Sunday. He is respected by our entire and surrounding communities, many of whom he has helped with good deeds, one way or another. Like our daddy, the boys drove the church bus to pick up those without transportation on Sundays as well and took them back home. This meant that most of their Sundays were busy doing those early-morning pickups, which they loved doing. They loved people too. Much like our Daddy, whom they copied in doing these and other helpful issues.

One of the stories I remember about my brother Buster as a child, is climbing onto the back of the couch where Buster was sitting and brushing his hair. He would hand me a brush while he and the rest of the family sitting on sofas and chairs were watching television. He would pay me a quarter when the show went off. I loved watching Buster and my other brothers sitting in the den or outside on the front porch in the summer months on Saturday afternoons, polishing their shoes. After cleaning the shoes with a soft brush, they began the process with much conversation amongst them.

The first layer was the black paste applied with a clean rag that Mama always made available to them. She knew the ritual, and had torn pieces of cloth for them. The boys would use it to shine the shoes. Then came the last ritual, buffing with a brush. They used black shoe polish to paint the soul of the shoes as the last step. I loved watching them all the time. I loved hearing how they kidded each other, one-up-man ship funny comments. Or even how they helped each other resolve problems. Saturday afternoons were great to me. Then they would all take baths, dress, and leave in their newly washed and shined cars for their dates. I learned the art of shining a shoe. I was impressed. So, when I got the same opportunity later on, I had good memories to keep the long process short. And hey, white shoe polish was nothing to mess with. Just saying.

As I grew older and as the brothers would set up the ironing board to press a shirt or pants for outings, I offered to help them to save them some time. For my little brother Junior, I offered to wash his laundry. While going through his jean pockets, I often found money left there. The money began happening more. I had told him what I had been finding, and he wanted me to keep it, as the reward for doing his laundry. When Mary and I came in for holiday visits, we always went out to Buster's barbershop to visit and harass him as much as possible. He always had customers waiting or in the chair, and he would stop and with a big grin, call us by nicknames. Of which no one had a clue in the shop of the origins. The three of us would laugh.

In his previous years, after going to serve our country in the Army, he moved to New Jersey for a time, where he received his barber's license. Buster is not afraid of work, and his clients over the years had grown. They'd grown so much over the decades, he had to "cut back" on what he could do in a week. In his earlier years, Buster, as an adult, worked at Broyhill, and while there purchased a 1957 Chevy. The car was black with a white tail fin. Lots of chrome. He'd "supe it up" later, adding a larger, more powerful motor. We could hear him coming home from his date every Saturday or Sunday. The ground felt like it was vibrating to the sound of his muffler. But Daddy and Mama did allow him to rush the motor prior to leaving for his dates, which emanated a loud roar. He'd do it a couple of times and we and our parents would laugh. He dated a lot in those days, as he had a car. But he finally settled down to some long-time dating sprees, ending up with the wife he has today, Fleeta.

Fleeta is a kind woman who strives to help others in the church as deaconess and Sunday school teacher. Her family is active in their churches as well. Buster has a high level of recognition in our community, due to his humble demeanor and willingness to help whenever he can. He and Fleeta have a son named Jessie Jr. Jessie Jr. has fathered two children, which made Buster and Fleeta grandparents.

Buster, Jim, and Pee-Wee and Bettye, who came up from Statesville, took turns to sit with Mama as she grew feebler. Daddy had his leg extracted and had to be placed in a care facility. I went home and saw him there. One day he was up and dressed in the clothing that Bettye had taken home to wash and bring back to his locker clean. Mama visited Daddy every day while he was there. When I was there, I drove her to see him. He soon passed away in a neighboring hospital. My sister Mary had flown in, and had planned to return to California and move back there to help him. But, while she was at the hospital, where she and Mildred and Hazel Mae sat with him, he passed away.

Mary said that she was talking to Daddy and he kept looking around. When she turned her back to him to turn on the television, and when she turned back to see what station he wanted to watch, he had quietly slipped away. The family was called. I returned there for the funeral. Mama passed away around six years later. But we decided that she would not be placed in a care facility. Thus began the rotation of the siblings to the house where we lived.

Pee-Wee stayed with her in spite of the other brothers coming for their turns. He had retired; the other two were still working. Junior always came on the weekends as soon as he parked his truck to be with Mama. Pee-Wee was the sibling who was sitting at the foot of her bed when she passed. The rest of us had been in other rooms, meeting people who wanted to come to say goodbye to Mama as she lay in her bedroom. She died on October 26, the anniversary of Daddy's parting this earth. However, his death came in June. Fleeta, Buster's wife, came often. And when Mama was up and getting around before becoming older and weak, Fleeta would take her to do her errands around town on a few occasions. Mama was buried alongside Daddy. Every time Mary, Thomas, and I visit North Carolina, we visit their gravesite, and we send flowers to place on the headstone on Mother's Day and Father's Day. Our brothers Pee-Wee and Jim would pick them up from Ms. Else on First Street in town, our pick as our family's florist, and place them there for the entire Mayes family as remembrance. Memories of them that we, and the family, and it seems the surrounding communities and towns, shall never forget.

Chapter 18:
Howard (Pee-Wee) Mayes

Pee-Wee holding flowers from Miss Elsie's shop for
Mama and Daddy's grave

The Jackie Gleason Show was one of the TV programs that we loved to watch at night when we were all sitting around in the den. We loved as a family watching shows like the westerns *The Lone Ranger, Rawhide, Bonanza*, and other shows like *I Love Lucy*. Pee-Wee was the Jackie Gleason of our family. Pee even imitated his little exit from the stage after Jackie came out in his bathrobe and scarf to thank the live audience who were cheering him. He would flex his arms up and down and exit with the phrase "And away we go!" Pee would use that phrase every time he exited our house. We would fall over laughing.

His sense of humor was a God-given gift. He used his humor in our family to diffuse arguments between us as siblings. He had a very tender heart as well, and maybe the gift of mercy from God too. After Pee married Hazel, his first wife, I'd drive up and spend a lot of time with them on weekends at their home in the mountains. It was a custom-built home, built after their marriage. The home was of a style of newer brick homes. It was so beautifully built with a large front yard and backyard, and the design inside was the new trend. In fact, their house, when completed, was highlighted in the town, and the house was open to the public for viewing one weekend. Two bedrooms, den, living room, and laundry. It was a showpiece of its day, and still holds that charm currently.

Howard (Pee-Wee) was a professional truck driver. He and Jim worked together for a former company named Champion. They hauled paper products, groceries in refrigerated trailers, and furniture. They hauled practically everything, with the exception of live animals like chickens. Their drives took a long time. Both of them were gone for a week, going to various places up and down the East Coast and inward. On occasion, they would take a longer trip, going to parts of California. Once Jim had a chance to do that and came to see me. Stupid me, I was so excited that I didn't have any food to give him. He was a gentleman, and stayed anyway.

Their work placed a hardship on their families. Their travels didn't leave much time to spend with them, especially during the week. So, you can imagine how they focused on home chores like mowing the grass, shopping for groceries, or even having family outings. However, they pulled it off. I saw that with my own eyes. I witnessed their love for their small children. Jim always had cookouts in the summer. Pee-Wee sat with his wife and watched the snow fall from their warm home. He also made phone calls to handle bills and other home-like issues. That made him very happy as I could see. Hazel was always happy he was home, of course. The kidding back and forth between them was hysterically funny. I visited them on Saturdays. Hazel would chase me away from the refrigerator, pretending that I couldn't have any of the food that they had put in there.

Tragically, Hazel was diagnosed with a brain tumor. After an operation to remove it, she was permanently paralyzed, and couldn't remember to form words. She sat speechless, and her sisters, who lived nearby, came to be with her as caregivers. Pee-Wee still had to go out on the truck to work, but on weekends he would come home and take Hazel with him shopping for groceries and other errands like banking. Hazel's condition never stopped her from trying. I learned over time that Daddy would go there practically every day, and talk to her and encourage her. That's when Hazel began her journey to healing. She returned to her old self with a very good sense of humor. Daddy spent many hours encouraging her to come out of her depression. He is the one who helped her walk again, and speak again. Pee-Wee was very happy telling me that story.

When I was there on weekends, I would pretend to be looking for food to eat in the refrigerator. She would protest by saying "What! What!" And come over to stand in front of the fridge to stop me from getting her food. We teased each other like this a lot. Unfortunately, I also messed up. Many times, Pee would drive Hazel down to "the house," as we referred to it. Hazel was there of course. When I was driving Hazel for whatever reason, I don't remember now, she wanted to go to inside the house. Well, she wore a metal brace to help her walk. She had often come inside with Pee. But he knew how to handle her, and he did with loving care all the time. He would help her up the stairs and into the house and then out after visits. Well, Hazel asked me to help her into the house. I got out of the car and helped her out. That went well. But! I couldn't help her like Pee did on the steps. And we both fell back with me landing on top of her.

I went into shock mode of seeing my death from Pee-Wee. You know what Hazel did? She fell out laughing, really hard. She was lying on the concrete walkway, laughing! I got up and helped her up and back into the car. Fortunately, she took up for me for the incident. She told Pee-Wee she wasn't hurt. Pee laughed too, and told me that episode was not the first time she had fallen. They both were laughing at this point, because over the course of time as she learned to walk again, she had fallen a lot.

Pee-Wee and Hazel were married for over twenty-nine years. The first three years were blissful before she and he went to find out why she was having migraine headaches. Hazel underwent two surgeries for tumors, and over time they grew back. The last time the doctors noted a tumor, Hazel decided that she wouldn't have another surgery. Pee supported her decision. And they lived as long as possible, knowing that her time wasn't long.

Her death came while sleeping. Pee called me to let me know in San Diego. I had grown very close to Hazel. Pee and I talked a long time; he was upset. After the phone call, I sat at my computer and wrote a poem about Hazel. I called Pee back later and read it to him. Pee decided that the poem would be a part of her obituary at the funeral. I couldn't come, but he called me and told me that the person who read the poem had read it like I had. And the reaction of the mourners was overwhelming. He said people were sobbing all over the congregation.

Then, he was no more. Our last conversation was over the phone. He had had a heart attack, and the fall left him paralyzed from the waist down. Pee had arteries blocked. Our family and Linda's family were torn up. Everyone was who knew him. The doctors operated and opened one of the arteries. Linda called to let me talk to Pee. He said in his usual funny ways, "I'm mad." I laughed and asked why. He said, "They won't let me have any chicken and pinto beans!" I laughed out loud. It was so good to get to talk with him again. That was when I found hope that he would live. I knew the situation of being paralyzed would factor into their lives. But I also knew that Pee had taken care of his first wife Hazel for over twenty-seven years. Then he told Linda to take the phone away. I was yelling at him by then, wanting to talk once more. He never came back.

A second operation was planned after he stabilized, to unblock the other artery. After the first operation, Pee recovered. In fact, he knew what had happened at home and how he came to be in the hospital. But just like his first wife did, and because he loved and trusted God to heal him, or help him, Pee took this in stride with his typical sense of humor and decided to overcome the condition. Linda drove the long drive every day to be with him, and in most cases stayed at her sister's house nearby. Pee had been sitting up the previous day with family who had come to visit him, laughing out loud at the cartoons. Pee loved watching cartoons, all day in fact. Junior had come to visit him, and as usual he was sitting up watching cartoons. Junior said he had sat with him, and they talked.

Linda, his wife of six years, was there too. She returned home just briefly to get some new clothing and to make arrangements at a rehabilitation facility, and Pee was fine. Linda is dearly loved by our family, as are her family. I remember driving her mom and Mama to her and Pee-Wee's house. I was shaking in my shoes. I was carrying precious cargo and drove as slowly as I could to get them there safely. I did with great relief. For Linda, her idea was to go home and return to the hospital.

The next day, on Sunday morning, Linda got a call from Pee's doctor saying he had coded. He'd had another heart attack and was code blue. Linda called me as she was driving a far distance to the hospital. She was distraught, and she couldn't find Buster, which made it worse. I told her to slow down and drive carefully. I told her that I would locate Buster and Jim to tell them what was happening. She wanted to know, as the doctor had asked her about resuscitation. I told her, after a minute, that since his quality of life would be worse, and the attempts to bring him back would in my opinion further harm him, that she should allow Pee to pass on. I learned later that she had put that question to Buster and Jim. Both agreed that Pee would not have a quality of life that even he could overcome.

The reason I told Linda Shae of my opinion to let him go was because I had been placed in a similar position here in California. A dear friend, Linda, and a prayer partner sister in the Lord, had to make this similar decision about her dearly beloved sister Lillian Taylor. Linda had called me around 1 a.m. to ask me to come to the hospital. I did immediately. She told me that the doctors wanted to know if Lillian coded, if the attempts to resuscitate would be enforced. Or, should the team of doctors and nurses allow her to pass without help or assistance. We talked again about the quality of life that Lillian would have ij she lived. After a while, Linda decided to have a conference with her doctors. Given the condition of Lillian at that time, no operation could save her life. And her chances of living through an operation were very low, around five percent.

So now, a few years later, I am in a similar position with my own sibling's wife. I knew that Linda Shae, my friend, had made the right decision concerning Lillian's health. Linda allowed Lillian to go into the arms of God. And I found that I felt the same way now about my brother Pee. I didn't want to have to deal with any more physical problems. And his condition was such that he would not have survived another operation. In fact, his body was beginning the process of shutting down after the latest heart attack.

Not being able to rouse Buster on the cell phone, I called and asked my cousin Mildred to get Buster or Jim, who were attending church nearby. She told me later that she had been recovering from a stroke, and hadn't gone out because she couldn't drive. But she drove her car to Macedonia church a short distance and connected with Buster and Jim. Then the boys with their wives drove to the hospital. But Pee was passing away.

Jim called me and Mary and comforted us afterward. We told Thomas, Mary's son. He was quiet. Every time the three of us went home to visit, Pee and Linda kept Thomas at their house, and Mary and I would stay at Bettye's and Russell's home in Statesville. Linda and Pee told Thomas that he was their son, and called him to talk or asked us how he was doing and sent their love to him. Thomas felt their love, and did feel like their son too. They would do all purchases for him on our visits. Thomas didn't ever worry about spending a dime.

Again, but in shock, the three of us flew home. The scene was totally different now. Sister Mom had passed on. Two weeks later Pee, who had just gotten home from a cruise with his family and his wife and Jim, was gone to Heaven. For Pee, I sometimes thought of his passing as mercy from God. He would have handled being paralyzed, and Linda had begun the process of finding a care facility for rehabilitation. Linda is so precious to us, as is her family Mary and Byron from Connecticut. When we arrived, we went to visit her. We helped with many facets of planning the funeral along with Byron and Mary, who had flown down immediately. Linda's sister Terry, and her husband Garland, were there as well, planning.

Pee was eulogized, and the most people I had ever known possible flocked to view him at Macedonia Baptist church. Hundreds upon hundreds came to also wait for the funeral. Linda held up, as that was one of her concerns, and we all prayed about that. Afterward, when we began the drive behind the hearse, we saw a city police car escorting Pee and family cars to the burial ground. Behind us was another city police car that followed up the procession. Cars pulled over with respect as we drove by. In the town, the main street was opened for us to go through. But! What struck me was that Pee, who must have had a great effect on many lives in town, had them now showing it in abundance.

Because other police officers stood at street entrances to the main one, they had blocked traffic from entering the main street where we were on. They stood outside their patrol cars as we and Pee processed by under police escort. The police standing at the entrance of the blocked streets had taken off their hats in respect to Pee and the family. Junior's stepson Justin was there also in his police uniform. Junior saw and looked his way and we waved at him. The hearse and family were escorted a long way to the burial grounds, some ten miles away. We later returned to a repass at Macedonia.

Let me tell you, it's hard when these life things happen. The boys still meet at the barbershop, and Jim's son Jamie helps more now with Jim around the church. Mary and Thomas returned to Los Angeles, as I returned to San Diego. We are still in shock. God will help us. The following is a poem that I had written for Pee's first wife Hazel, whom we dearly loved. As I said before, it was met with great compassion and grief for the family and church after being read. Here it is:

<u>My Poem to Hazel: the first wife's eulogy</u>

"It Was a Good Day to Pass Away"

It was a good day to pass away.

The leaves had turned red, gold, orange, and some green was left on the corners, just to let you know that there had been Some life, once.

It was a good day to pass away.

The air was cool enough to see the impression of your breath

Made as it curled out of your mouth. Not yet frosty cold,

Not yet.

On occasion, a bit of warm air would swirl around to try to

Encase the cooler air, just enough

To remind the cool air that there was still a little life left,

In the passing summer.

It was a good day to pass away.

The children still play in the park, not wanting the season of

Freedom to end.

Let's slide once more down the shiny glide, into the dirty pit.

Oh! At the end of those rainy, wet days,

It had been the best way to lunge down the long twisting slide,

Into the cool of the muddy water.

It was a good day to pass away.

People would go about their way to church that morning.

The sun would be up in the sky, shining bright, and golden.

Burning the cold wet dampness of the morning dew away.

Yes, it would be a good day today.

I knew, you know.

I had known for quite some time.

Way back, far back. A long time ago

Back when They told me that I would not last,

Pass a certain Time.

I knew that They had been wrong though,

About my certain time.

I knew that there would be a time.

Just as Certain as I knew that the Sun would come up and dry

The cold dampness from the air, from the leaves,

After I had gone.

I knew.

That Someone other than Them would decide.

It was a good day to pass away.

My friends were saying hello and goodbye.

We had laughed Hard.

We almost laughed ourselves to death,

At some silly story my husband had told.

In our joy, in my joy, we knew.

We knew it would be a good day too.

But so soon?

I have laid with my husband, on this bed. Our Bed of Memories.

Tears.

Hopes.

Sorrow.

Dreams.

Plans made, some achieved.

Pledges broken.

Joy.

Laughter.

Love,

I lay with my husband, here; now. While he sleeps,

Peacefully.

I remember. I remember all of it, I smile.

I know that he'll remember too. And will smile.

Oh yes. Yes. Yes, it was.

It was a good day, to pass away.

Howard, a few years later met and dated Linda Parks and got married in 2005 at Macedonia Baptist Church. They were very happy and flew out to San Diego on their honeymoon. They visited the ultimate warship Pee-wee and Linda spent quality time together with family and friends. Linda calls their residence location "Mayes mountain." She is originally from Wilkesboro, North Carolina.

Linda Mayes? Our family still treats her as our sister. Because she is, as well as her family. We all talk often, and communicate in various ways. She and Fleeta do breakfasts together. Linda attends her namesake church, Parks, in Wilkesboro, North Carolina. She organizes events, and leads the local committees on personal projects.

Linda is working hard with a group of people, in an effort in Wilkesboro, North Carolina, to restore Lincoln High School. She asks people for donations to support the restoration. Our family's tie-in with that is that our ancestor's, Mammy Judy's, legacy is being renewed too. Elizabeth Grinton, a descendant of Mammy Judy, was a teacher at Lincoln. Elizabeth put on a one-woman show at Wilkes Community College. Our Mama was the descendant of Sue, one of Mammy Judy's daughters. See the details on Mammy Judy's lineage in her chapter. My hope and prayer is that Linda, who is following in my ancestors' footsteps, will be successive. I will know.

Pee-Wee's obituary:

Pee-Wee, AKA Jackie Gleason, is deceased. He was a graduate of Happy Plains High School. His first job was at a furniture factory on an assembly line dealing with cushions. After a few years, he decided to become a truck driver. A firm that was a mile or so down a road piqued his interest. He was allowed to drive a truck around the company's yard. The interest in this realm remained. So, he applied for to a new company called Champion Paper. He and our other brother James worked there for decades. He was a lifetime member of Macedonia Baptist Church. The same one we all attended and still attend for a few of them. Pee-Wee was on the board of trustees, and an usher, and a member of an all-male choir. He got up early on Sunday mornings and drove the church van to pick up members who couldn't attend due to transportation issues or having no license to drive. He was married to Linda Parks, whom he referred to as "sweetie" for eight years. James (Slim) Mayes, number four. James, or Jim, partnered with Pee-Wee as a professional truck driver. He has four children and one grandchild. He is married to Jean. He too graduated from Happy Plains High School. He is now retired, but working part-time at a trucking firm. Decades after retirement, Howard (Pee-Wee) passed away.

END

Linda and Pee-Wee visiting California with me, Mary, and Thomas at Sea Port Village on the bay

Chapter 19:
James Mayes

Jim with Mama at one of the family's favorite restaurant, and we were all there with Mama and with nieces and nephews in tow!

As I write this section, Jim is being released from the hospital after a minor stroke (TIA). By the time you see this information, Jim would have been at home, but not back to work. There is no reason to fear, as he will live a long life. And he is healthy. So, I want to tell you about my big brother, Jim. Slim is my nickname for him. Slim often acknowledged his fitness that he always cared about. But! He had a weakness: pepper.

At the dinner table, he would use it to the point where anyone sitting near him would start snickering. I told you earlier how when he entered the kitchen when he still lived there, he would flex his muscles and grin wide like a kid. And he did develop big muscles. He and his brothers were well aware of keeping fit, and they even entered a competition among themselves to see which one was the strongest. Endless contests, even up until the day they left our home to live their own life.

Jim and Pee were the ones I ran around with. When he and Pee-Wee returned home on the weekend from the truck, I would drive Pee's car to their terminal, which was located just a few miles around the corner. They would blow the big horn of the truck if they were coming home in the middle of the night. I mean that no matter the time, I had to take the car to them to pick them up. For some reason, Jim was the brother to whom I talked to if I was having a problem or issues. When he was settled at home, I'd call him, or go to see him at his house.

He had married years prior of course, first to Susan Jones. They had three children who are now grown and doing GREAT. They are Jamie, Donna, and Wendy. Jamie (I call him James) graduated college with a degree as a teacher. He received awards every year as teacher of the year. Upon visiting the Mayes compound, I'd visit him and see the awards he had received from the school. He has retired, and has come out to visit us a couple of times by road trip.

Wendy is working on her master's degree. She has a son named Deion. He is very successful in his profession. Donna has birthed three children, and one of them has birthed one, which makes

Donna a grandmother. Wendy has one son who has made a great life with his own family. In my times there, I actually babysat these nieces and nephew. I did so for Jessie Jr., who was a baby at the time. Jessie's aim was very accurate, as I attempted to put a diaper on him. He would laugh as he tried to spray me with another shot of urine, even in a perfect arch.

Jim's new wife after the divorce is Jean. She is the best cook outside my Mom and Mary I have ever tasted. We made a bee-line to her and Jim's house every time we came home. We did the same with Pee-Wee's wife, Hazel. The Parsons, Hazel's sisters, made the best cakes in the world. I didn't know a cake could be so tall. There's is like the one at Claim Jumper, multiple layers. Daddy told them to bake cakes for our Christmas. The Parson sisters baked coconut cake, and chocolate cakes for us. Those cakes were our family favorites. Daddy picked them up from their house. The Parson sisters baked cakes for Christmas season for gifts to others. I don't think the ones who received those cakes were ever unhappy. The Parson family attended church together every Sunday, with full outfits, gloves, and hats. That is the tradition there and in the surrounding committees and towns. In Taylorsville alone, there are large churches along the main street, and on the back as well. Majestic churches. And the citizens eagerly attended.

Again, we still keep the Parson family in our hearts. Just because Hazel passed didn't mean that we cut off communication with the family. I often called the sisters when I lived there. I also came to the house too to visit.

Jean and Jim did a masterful job operating a food wagon for early workers at their plant. Their food sold out quickly, and the two of them would increase their numbers to cover all the needs. Jim and Jean have been active in church at Macedonia Baptist church. Jim ushered and was a trustee, and Jean supported programs and events of the church. And of course, between Mill, Hazel Mae, and

Caldonia, our cousins, food was exceptional. Jean brought food to our Christmas and Thanksgiving dinners at the house, and sometimes at Sister Mom's house in Statesville, North Carolina. We numbered in the twenties with all of us and family friends.

James (Jim), Jessie (Buster), and Howard (Pee-Wee)

Jim is the person I can talk to and get answers and support from as I said before. His quiet demeanor and wisdom were birthed in Mama and Daddy's house. Jim, after his final retirement, was able to assist others in the community. He and Jean have had a wonderful marriage. Jean has helped her family many times during the rigors of life, and is wise in her thoughts and actions. Jim was the one, who along with Pee-Wee and Jamie, would work at the church. Every weekend, he and Pee completed a list of church projects set out in a list. Chores like clean the church bathrooms and repair anything not working, making sure the grass was cut, and other issues relayed to them. Of course, Jim took his turn with Mama as she was declining in health.

Jean came very often too. Jean has a job helping people who are aged. Jim at one point decided to return to work as a truck dock guide and on occasion drives the trucks a short distance as a replacement sometimes for a driver who didn't get in. But again, after the minor stroke, he retired completely. Remember that he, Pee, and Junior were in some cases still professional truck drivers. He was in a truck when he had a mini stroke. He is better, and is on the mend. He had his mini stroke at the same time he was off work, home helping Jean, who had full knee replacement surgery a few days past. So, they were in a situation that would come to prove that God would sustain them.

Jim was funny. While in the hospital, he told his brother, Buster, to stop reporting on him. Apparently, Buster had told the town about the incident, and Jim said people were coming to see him and calling him on the cell very concerned. Oh well, all has turned out perfect. He was sent home, and his son James drove him. This isn't the only test for Jean and Jim. A couple of years ago, they lost Jean's son by another marriage. Her son, Jonathan, was in his church choir. I was told that he was very active in his church. He had been in the military, and had served in Vietnam. He was beloved by many.

As I said before, Jim and I talked more. Once on a visit for business in the state, he took me on one of his truck routes. We drove through turning and falling leaves. This was during the time that the leaves were turning, and they were all fall colors. We were the only ones on the road, I kid you not. And it was gorgeous. He drove and talked, and I listened. I talked and he listened for hours. He stopped at a picnic area with an upper roof and picnic tables underneath. I took lots of pictures and sent them back to Mama to show her and Jim. Cameras are very important to me. Daddy took pictures everywhere. He was the one that gave me my own camera. It was a small camera, but it worked. It used film, which Daddy provided. Jim took pictures too with his camera, and he videotapes too. So, between Daddy, Jim, and myself, we had every angle covered. We all had fun doing it. Plus, some like Pee-Wee would go into a funny dialogue, and had everybody cracking up laughing. Oh Lord, we had fun at our gatherings. Paradise on earth.

When I worked at a research laboratory with the federal government for the Navy for over thirty-five years, one of my tasks was what I loved. I got to videotape meetings and a few conferences at the site. I took pictures as well for the center via my branch manager, Tom Schlosser, one of two supervisors who were excellent to work for. He gave me a blog site under the military code of ".mil" to place the pictures and write articles on the scientists' and system managers' creations for consumption of new technology being done there and at other laboratories. So, I would interview these people in the areas of their expertise, and write the article on my blog called "Bessie's Blog." I had many followers in the upper echelon and other places around the nation reading and commenting on the reports. But! I loved taking pictures, as does Jim. I did that for years before being moved to another assignment in the branch.

I kept the blog as active as I could with new material pertinent to the mission of SPAWAR SYSTEMS CENTER. On the ship, I purchased a hat with the call signs of USS active members. I didn't realize just how many people of Florida knew the Navy. Another "duh" moment for me. I gave it to Pee, who wore it proudly because of the word "Navy" on it. My brother Jim advised him NOT to wear it anymore while they were in Florida. Why? The experienced and retired Navy community kept asking him which division he served in. What a story. Working with military and civilian personnel, it never occurred to me that the active community would want to honor him for his service to the country. Yikes! So, Pee did stop wearing it. But Pee and my brothers and sisters served this country in a different way, and were honored for that service. No harm, no foul.

Another ship beside the USS *San Diego*

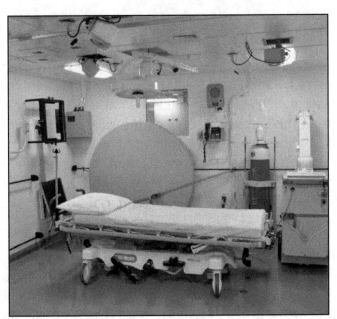

Hospital room on USS *San Diego* LPD 22

But in regard to Pee-Wee he took me on rides in the mountains around where he and Hazel lived. He went the route he had taken when he was dating Hazel. We ended up at a road that had a sign not to enter. This puzzled Pee, since the gate was normally open. But! Pee knew the owner and commented he would go to his house to get permission to be on his property. And so, we did. It was a very bumpy road, but we did reach the owner's house, which happened to be out in his apple orchid. As Pee got out of his truck, the owner came forward.

Pee told his friend with the largest house I had ever seen in Taylorsville that he wanted to show his sister where the hang gliders pushed off the top of the mountain. Pee introduced me to his friend and they talked a while. Later as Pee drove through the apple orchard with red apples ready to be picked, I thanked God for the beauty in that place. Apples as far as the eye could see. Beautiful apples; no bugs had defaced them. And was amazed at my brother's range of friends. He knew this man!!

This brought back memories of the orchards that belonged to the Hinshaws that had been planted in the fields in back of our house. When we were children, we would play among them. We also picked the apples while we were there and ate them on the spot. I preferred the Red Delicious and Roma apples. There were so many varieties that you could eat, different ones every day, and never repeat for weeks. This orchard was behind our house, but Hinshaw had another orchard in the fields behind his house. So, we would go there to get other varieties before they were all picked. That field yielded Golden Delicious apples. Oh my, my, my. Listen, I thanked God for the bounty that surrounded our home, where we could make pies from the Granny sour apples. Or pick the strawberries that grew under one of the trees, for which Mama would make strawberry pie. However, this trek through the site of the hang gliders got a little scary for Pee and me.

There were hang gliders there jumping off the top of this mountain. Pee and I watched as they prepped their gear and got into a good position to fly. There were three men who were doing these flights. They belonged to a hang gliders club and used that area with the permission of the owner to fly down to the meadow below, he told Pee. Pee was fascinated by the whole process, as was I. I had my camera, of course. I took shots of the men getting the gear up, backing up, and running to jump straight off the mountain. One after one jumped. And I clicked and clicked and clicked again. I was having a field day!

Now, let me just say here about a time that I frightened my brother Jim when we were in the mountains riding around. We also had stopped at another spot that overlooked a mountain. There was a log there that basically said don't go beyond the barrier. Well, I wanted to see the valley, and I stepped over it. I happened to look back at my brother Jim, who had a terrified look on his face. I took a quick glance and stepped back to the barrier and to a safe spot. He told me later that my antics did make him very uneasy. So now here I am, watching the gliders jump off the mountain. And so, they did. Professional gliders.

Pee and I watched as the last one launched, and walked to almost the ledge. We saw how their canopy filled with wind and floated down to the valley below. I was still taking pictures of this. I wanted to get a picture of them landing in the valley, and I walked to the very edge of the mountain to watch them. I lost my balance at the edge and used my arms to steady myself so I would not fall. Pee saw this, and as I walked back from the edge, he lightly scolded me. He said that I could have fallen off the mountain, and at that point, he would drive down into the valley and pick up my body. I love my brothers and always respect their opinions. I also accept being corrected by them for my actions. Needless to say, Pee was done, and we left and went back down the mountain and home.

From our front porch, overlooking one of Hinshaw fields used to grow hay for their horses

Pee on the front porch after a small freeze occurred overnight

Jim graduated from our local school Happy Plains. His work for the church is appreciated by the members of Macedonia, and they look to him and Jamie now if anything goes awry. Oh, by the way, Jim has cut down on his pepper.

As a parent, I know of Jim's deep love for his family. I can't highlight all of their many accomplishments in both education and personal. However, I don't think they'll mind if I do so for their older brother "Jamie."

Education and Certifications:

Master of Arts Educational Media
Concentration: Instructional Technology Specialist Computers
Appalachian State University, NC 2007

Computer Education Endorsement-079
Appalachian State University, NC 2007

Master of Arts United States & World History
Appalachian State University, NC 1999

Bachelor of Science Social Studies (Grades 9-12)
Appalachian State University, NC 1992

88091 – Special Education: General Curriculum Endorsement
00760 – Vocational Business Education (6-12) Endorsement

Teaching Achievements:

2015 Catawba Rosenwald School Teacher of the Year
2014 Catawba Rosenwald School Teacher of the Year
2010 Catawba Rosenwald School Teacher of the Year
2009 Catawba Rosenwald School Teacher of the Year
2007 Catawba Valley High School Teacher of the Year
2006 Catawba Valley High School Teacher of the Year
2005 Catawba Valley High School Teacher of the Year
2002 Hickory Public School Teacher of the Year
2002 Catawba Valley High School Teacher of the Year
2000 Catawba Valley High School Teacher of the Year
1996 Catawba Valley High School Teacher of the Year
Appalachian State University, Phi Alpha Theta History Honor Society

Chapter 20:
Mary Mayes: My constant roommate

Mary and I shared a room much of our lives when we lived in Taylorsville as young children. So, our closeness in future events was good because we kind of understood each other. However, she and I had totally different personalities. She was the one who moved from Charlotte and eventually to California. She was our longest explorer, going all the way "to the end of the country," per Mama. So, Mama and I flew to see her on the week of July 4th almost every year. I followed Mary with as much interest as I had my other siblings in Taylorsville. All fascinated me with their mannerisms and personalities. I, to this day, am very appreciative of their wiliness to teach me about life. She married a man who is the father of her son Thomas, John Harper.

Harper was a businessman and entrepreneur, and was very active politically in his community. He owned a cab company and was the lead in getting more cabs involved in getting licenses. At that time, the market had been monopolized by the Yellow Cab Company. The Yellow Cab Company was massively global, and was the standard by which other cab companies were to operate. The cities in San Diego utilized Yellow Cab at their venues, which squeezed out the competition in large swabs of areas. Also, their cabs were the first ones you would see leaving an airport or a hotel. They lined up in front of these types of high-traffic businesses, and more than made out with business profits for drivers and corporate. So, John Harper went to the city council to argue his case against this preferential treatment given by the city and other governing bodies throughout the state. After many attempts, and a city council that finally couldn't deny the truth, he won.

Just by doing that, he broke the chokehold, or monopoly, that the Yellow Cab Company had held for decades. To this day, cab companies both small and large benefit from his tireless efforts. With John watching, the city council made the cabs line up in a queue, which meant that Yellow Cab had to wait its turn along with private cab companies. Also, and more importantly, Yellow Cab could no longer purchase all the permits, which was leaving their competition with little choice but to operate with the few they were allowed. With John's efforts, new rules placed no limits on the number of licenses available that cabs could acquire. Over that first year, you noticed that a lot more cabs, using colors other than yellow, were on the road. John's cab name was Blue Cab. His motto on his cab fleet was "Go with Blue." Cab permits/licenses could be sold or passed on to other cab firms.

Unfortunately, John died after a long illness, leaving Mary with their son. According to Mary, John chose that name for their son because of John's close relationship with his brother named Thomas. Thomas, the son, who acts just like his intelligent father, attended a private Catholic school during his elementary days. He then attended another private school from which he graduated called La Jolla Country Day. He also was accepted and graduated from the prestigious Whittier College, where President Nixon and other leaders attended. He received a degree in psychiatry. Thomas is currently working with an organization for the poor called People Assisting the Homeless (PATH) as manager of a team. And just like his father John and his mother Mary, Thomas's heart has always been toward the neediest among our world. He demonstrated that to me before he actually joined PATH.

He had taken to making sandwiches for the homeless, and handing them out at night around Los Angeles. He volunteered at the PATH homeless shelter, and was so good and effective, the director hired him and then promoted him twice. Once as case manager, and then to work with the homeless in finding proper living to get them off the streets in Los Angeles. The director, who is joined by Hollywood celebrities, ministers, and local leaders, sits on the board.

In 2018, the board shifted the goal of the organization to helping house veterans living on the street. Thomas, as one of their managers, and his teams work hard at this. Part of their goals and responsibilities was having to set up the homeless housing, and checking on those who survived the war, but not what happened afterward. PATH provided clothing and food and helped the homeless receive benefits through the many state, federal, and local governments. And as they make the necessary steps to renew their lives and abide by the organizational rules, they are assigned housing with vouchers. The organization itself has a high profile in Los Angeles, where Thomas lives.

Thomas's love for those in need mirrors the values that Mary as a strong, mature Christian woman taught him growing up. His father Harper passed away as a Christian as well, having been led to Jesus by Mary. So, he too had the same Godly Christian values in his heart when he became a Christian early in his life. His cousins love him as does the entire Mayes family. In fact, as you would recall from Pee-Wee's and his wife Linda's profile, Thomas was the son they adopted, and they kept in touch with him. And they spoiled him. They could do no less. And neither could the whole family.

My son too, Thomas!

She left North Carolina and moved to California during the '70s. Her goal was to travel the world, but marriage and the birth of a blessed son happily placed it on hold. Years later, she traveled to Europe and the Holy Land in Israel. Mary is currently pursuing a master's degree in global business and leadership at Regent University. She serves in the Ministry of Helps as a greeter at her local church, and a volunteer with the Friends of University of California in Los Angeles (UCLA) Extension.

Chapter 21:
Harvey Mayes Junior

My hero li'l brother at Mama's house to see her, Mary, and me

My little brother embarrassed me by getting married first! That's how I felt when he married his wife Diana. I did get over it, though, and he had two children: Harvey III and Angela. Our Mama and daddy practically reared them as well. They were around six and seven when they both were brought into the house to live after Diana decided she would not care for them. His job didn't allow him to be home during the week. So, when he did come to be with them at the house, their time together when he was off the truck was well spent.

I'll tell you about the red sleigh. Although my brother and Diana did divorce, his life didn't stop. He recovered moved on. Junior is very intelligent and is very interested in politics. His life as a professional truck driver has been difficult on him and his family. But what I noticed, and what Mama told me, was that his children respected him. And when disciplinary action was necessary, he dealt it out to them when at home. He told me that he didn't like doing that, as he didn't want to be considered an ogre on the few days he was home with them. But, he did it for their sake and the sake of Mama and family.

As I had left the home by then and lived in California, I didn't see how things played out. He did resume a serious relationship. But my memories of Junior were more in how we grew up in the house, as we were the only ones left after the other siblings had gotten married or moved away. Dynamics change, but basic personalities don't.

As a kid, Junior's only desire for the entire year was to get a red sleigh for sledding. And he did. I was aware of there being "no Santa" due to my ruthless—uh—I mean older sister Mary, who told me one Christmas that Daddy and Mama were Santa. It took me a long time to forgive her. But my regret was that I told Junior that during a time when he should have had at least one more Christmas still believing that Santa was real. No one in our family had ever asked for such an expensive gift. And his trust that he could have one even impressed me. I know that Mama and Daddy were disappointed in me too. He was the last in the line of siblings that would have that glow of believing in Santa Claus. He did get a chance to ride it as a kid. And I still regret telling him about the fact that Santa didn't exist afterward. I can remember his face, because he is very intelligent and a very deep thinker. He took that information and asked our parents if it was true. They had to say yes.

Normally when we got snowstorms as children, we disassembled cardboard boxes to make runs down the hill beside our house, or behind the Hinshaw house on a long downhill in their woods. Daddy also took him sleighing on a back road beside the dime store, which had longer, steeper hills. Having a real red sleigh for Christmas for Junior made us very happy for him. Even me.

As I said before, Junior works as a long-haul professional truck driver. After he and Diana divorced, he took up the care of the two children, and Mama and Daddy helped him to rear them. Mama would go to the high school to see Junior play as a star receiver. He scored many touchdowns for the school. In fact, Junior broke the school record for touchdowns. He was someone other teams had to plan against to win. His son Harvey III also played football, as a defensive end. Mama said that she always yelled for him when he got the football to "run!" As the youngest of Junior's children, he excelled in his senior year as a player.

Prior to Mama and Daddy rearing them, my parents and I were the only ones living there in the house for many years. I left for California to live with my sister Mary. Junior still drives trucks, but has established his own clientele to whom he delivers goods. He and his partner Rhonda live on the Mayes compound in a home near Jessie and Fleeta and James Jr. Our Mama and daddy left all seven of us two and one-half acres each to build a home on—the same place near where Daddy had grown his tobacco crop.

We talk more since the death of our two siblings. They had died of health conditions two weeks apart. We who are left are still devastated. We were all so close. We talked to each other a lot, as Bettye was in the lead of the family, being the eldest. But, after their deaths, we have stayed in touch even more so. Much more.

Whatever Bettye told us what to do, we knew to do it as she was the spokeswoman for the family via Daddy and Mama. Buster would tease her a little. But she spoke for Daddy and Mama, and we did as told.

An example would be when Mama ordered the spring cleaning for the main house. Junior and I were still living there. But all the married or unmarried and living-alone brothers would return to help. The boys had the yards where Daddy told them what to do. Mary, Bettye Mama, and I had the inside. We threw clothing that had not been used in years out the upstairs windows. The women washed the windows inside the house and cleaned out the cupboards, cleaned underneath the cabinets, and did a thorough cleaning of the bathroom, for example. At the end, the house was clean, the curtains and windows were washed, and Mama and Daddy were pleased. We all gathered outside in the yard, talked a little while, then returned to our different places. We were happy too.

Buster (Big Bro) is in charge of the family now. He calls us every Sunday, just like Bettye called every Saturday to get information on what was going on in our lives or needs and would then give that information to the other siblings. Nowadays, Buster is that contact person as head of the family. Even Junior is contacted no matter where he is. He and Buster live in the same community. We call Junior and the others too.

Again, as close as we were, the passing of our other siblings, one expected and the other not, moved us in ways one can't explain. Junior in particular was affected. He, Pee-Wee, and Jim would meet at Buster's barbershop every weekend before customers and talk. Then the other brothers, not Buster, would go off to do errands, or work at Macedonia during necessary repairs or cleaning up. Since Junior had only a couple days off, he did errands around his house. He is our Little Brother, a name we call him when he calls. And he is a very good father and a very good man. He reared two families that came together under his roof that included Rhonda's daughter's family. Their mother, Rhonda's daughter Paula, passed unexpectedly. Such a tragic time for Junior. Junior has had a few very sad incidents prior to Sister Mom passing. He lost his nephew DJ, his daughter's other son, to an accidental drowning. He fell out of a canoe into a raging current.

DJ was out with his friends when this happened. DJ was living a wonderfully successful life. He was a supervisor at the place of his work. He had a girlfriend and would have had an even better future before this happened. Junior said to me that Tuesdays were becoming a day that he expected to hear bad news. With Sister Mom going a while after, this pretty much devastated him, he told me. Then more inexplicitly, Pee-Wee. He is recovering, albeit slowly. We all are recovering slowly.

We are very close, the Mayes. The reason: our parents taught us the ways of God. No matter how long it took us to accept Jesus, we all did. And their legacies are in this book. I have had great success due to following Jesus and his way. The time here in California has been hard at times, but I have very close friends, some of whom have become actual family. One is Ada. Ada Fabish and her mother, Velda, were close too. Mama had a picture of the two of them hanging on her bedroom wall. Velda and my mom became friends when Mama was out visiting. They became very close after that, with both asking about each other. Ada has been our sister, even before she buried her mother.

Velda and Ada with me and Mama at a restaurant in San Diego, CA

Chapter 22:
Bessie Mayes; Out of the ashes of Hell to triumph

I'm placing myself as the last chapter of this memoir. My walk with God, in this book, may be more difficult to take for some readers. Plus, I want the reader to understand the type of home I grew up in. And the type of siblings I adore and love being around. My mom and dad give a taste of the type of home we, as siblings, loved living in and the environment that God created for us. As John said about Jesus, books cannot hold everything He did for us while He lived on the earth. I'm not saying that anything I do can come close to outdoing Jesus's ministry. However! I do understand the fact that not all we experienced in our family can ever be written down here. So, I wanted to allow you to experience my chapter at the end of the book. The setting of my life for us siblings, and what happens to me in this chapter, will draw the contrast to a degree. I loved my life growing up. And what our parents modeled for us. God helped me to cope after what happened to me. So here I am.

God is trusting and loving:

I was very happy during my teen years. My birthday is in the hottest month of the season in North Carolina. It was during this time that I also met friends at their houses throughout the town. In my younger years, Daddy or Mama would send me out to friends' homes to show them love, and inspire them to come to church. It worked ninety-nine percent of the time. If Uncle Harve and Miss Lucille felt safe with their daughter, then that touched. And I did behave. But I remember being at a friend's house on a Saturday afternoon. I went there often. Her father worked at night cleaning businesses. So, we had to be quiet.

I remembered on another occasion her father and brother carried in her older brother, who was totally drunk. About that time, there had been an incident where her older brother had been accused of raping a nurse. He had spent time in jail until bail was set, which his father paid. I couldn't understand how this happened, but then I didn't know this one like I knew his younger siblings. My friend was a class above me, and the others were either the same age as me or slightly older. It was during this period of my life that I really felt free and happy. I could go to places that my dad and mom approved of. Meet with people they approved of too. I had been at this house in particular to spend time with my friend. My parents had approved of this because they knew the family. They were very careful as to where I would go and who I was with, how I would get there and return.

So, during this period I had just entered junior high school, and my friend and I knew each other from there. She had begged me to come to her house on Saturdays. My parents seemed a little concerned. I noticed that but didn't give it much thought at the time. Now I know that it was because they too had knowledge of the alleged rape by the older brother on the nurse. She dropped the charges at the last minute, due to her being shamed in the town by townsfolk. The rape had occurred at night at the hospital. I assume it was because the older brother had been taken there for treatment due to high levels of alcohol in his body. I think he was banned from ever coming back there, thus his being carried in by his father and brothers. They seemed quite unfazed by this. My conclusion was that the brother did this often. As he lay in this bedroom, he yelled for aspirin. The father refused to give him one. He said it was to punish him for getting drunk. He yelled most of the day, but his yelling was ignored by family members.

By this time, my visits there were commonplace on Saturday. One night, my friend and I were at a small nightclub in a neighboring town. Her elder brother happened to be there too. We were about to leave when he approached us. Although my friend was driving, I wanted to stay there a little longer. Her brother said that he could take me home. My friend Emma looked very concerned and asked me, "Are you sure?" Since I had been to their house many times and had interacted with all her brothers, I saw no harm in it and said I was sure. So that night, he drove me home along with some of his adult friends.

When we arrived at the place he lived, I said, "I thought you were taking me home." The others, by this time, had passed out from drinking too much alcohol. He said for me to come to his house, and that I could make a telephone call to my parents. I had no reason to suspect anything else, given that I had known this family and trusted that all was well with them. So, he led me into his house. When we got there, I asked him where his phone was so that I could call home. The room was dark, so I asked him to turn on the light so I could see the numbers. That is when he grabbed me from behind.

We both struggled. I was trying to get away from him, because he was trying to subdue me. I began to scream as loudly as I could, and at the same time fight him off. My brothers had taught me to defend myself, and I employed those techniques. For a while I was winning. Still screaming for help, I almost got free. That is when he began to choke me so he could prevent my screaming for help and control me. He said, "Stop screaming and I won't choke you." Really, I couldn't scream at that point because he was choking me tighter. In fact, I could feel myself at the point of passing out. My thought was at that moment that he was about to rape me. I also decided that it wasn't worth dying, that I could tell people what happened later. He stopped choking me. But I decided to continue to struggle with him. I was still thinking I could get away from this horrible situation. But I couldn't stop him from the rape. He raped me. He threw me down on the bed and forced himself on top of me.

All my life, I had a goal not to become involved with any man sexually. My desire was to wait for marriage, and let my husband be the first. I felt the moment my virginity was shattered. I was, at that point, mad at myself for not thinking. For allowing myself to be misled so easily. Then I became angry at myself, again, to be taken in by someone I thought was okay. As this violation continued, I cried. It was extremely painful.

Later, he led me sobbing all the way back to the car. But it was gone. He then flagged down a passing car that held a number of people. He got in the car and pulled me in too. He sat beside me as they drove me home. He had his arm around me in a way that made it appear that we were together on purpose. I should have told them; I should have screamed again out loud and ran away. But I didn't do any of those things. I was still in shock and shamed because of what had just happened to me. I remember to this day how those men looked at time. I bent over a number of times because I was ashamed and didn't want to be seen. I did this a couple times on the way to my home.

When we turned into my driveway, the men in the car said that they could take me further up the path, but I declined. As I got out of the car, that thing said to me, "I'll call tomorrow." I left the car, still in shock, and in a lot of pain from the rape. As I entered the house, I went to the bathroom. I just wanted to wash everything that had just happened to me. I couldn't look at myself in the mirror. When I disrobed, I noticed that my panties were bloody in the seat. I knew from others that when you lose your virginity on the night of your marriage, that there would be blood that indicated that you were a virgin. I looked at the blood in the bottom of the seat of the panties. I said, "He took my virginity. Now I won't be able to have my husband do that for me on our wedding night. It's gone forever, and there was nothing I could. I will never get it back."

I cleaned myself up, trying to erase any parts of him left on my body. I didn't sleep; I couldn't sleep. I felt ashamed, stupid. I thought, "He had raped me like he did that nurse." It was true that he had raped her. It was all true.

Afterward, my attitude toward my parents and anyone else changed. I felt alone and soiled. I couldn't face them with what happened. I called my friend Rebecca and told her what had happened. I could tell she was very upset and angry. She wanted me to call the police department and report it. It was at this point I realized something else. I couldn't call the police to tell them. All the policemen in our little city knew both my father and mother. In fact, they were very close. The police had asked Daddy to tell me to stop running through the yellow lights. And Daddy did. Rest assured that I didn't do that again because I knew they were watching.

I felt too ashamed at my stupidity and the fact that I didn't want to harm Daddy's and Mama's reputation. I had seen how the townspeople had derided the nurse for reporting her rape. Even the police wondered if she had done something to bring it on, I was told. How could I report that if no one would believe me? Again, I felt hopeless. I told Rebecca that I couldn't. I was the one who broke their number one rule. "Return with the same people you left with." That was because they had approved the people I was going to be with at the time. Again, I felt the shame of disobedience and stupidity for breaking that cardinal rule. All these reasons were flying around in my head. All I wanted was an escape from the horror of what had just happened to me. This is why I couldn't, wouldn't admit what had happened to me. Little did I know that I would live to regret that decision.

After a few days had passed and we were in the next weekend, I received a telephone call from Glen, the one who had raped me. He wanted me to come to the woods to meet him. I was in a panic. I sat down on the couch arm. I became faint. He told me that he would tell my father and mother what had happened if I didn't show up. These woods were near our home. As a child, I would walk the path that led to the next neighborhood. It was a shortcut. My aunt still lived in a house on the opposite of the forest, which was why I used the path to get to her home. I begged him not to tell my parents. He shouted, "Then you meet me in the woods!" I realized months later that since I had not reported the rape, that he had gotten off. Had I done that, instead of another rape occurring, the police would have used that for a sting.

I cried. I was horrified that I would ruin my parents' reputations in the community. I made the decision that I had to go to shut him up from telling anyone about what he had done to me. Of course, I hadn't again, because of the way the townspeople treated the nurse badly who had reported her rape by this creature. She wouldn't press charges. I think that was because she would have to testify on the stand in public. After that rape, I believe she just couldn't deal with it anymore. So, I went to the woods. He had told me that he was bringing a gun. I should not have gone. I should have reported what had happened to them and the police department. But I felt I had no other choice. I was desperate that Mama and Daddy's reputation in the community not be ruined by my disobedience to the rules.

Again, he raped me. You may have thought that what I was doing at that moment was insane; you would be correct. This decision wasn't made by someone who was sane at that time. That decision was being made by someone who just turned fourteen, a teenager. That decision was made by someone who thought that no boy would ever date me again after they had learned what had happened. That I would be considered tainted goods, not a proper wife to have their child. That decision was made by someone who thought that this would be the last call.

After he raped me again, I begged him not to tell my parents. He said he wouldn't. How stupid, right? I am begging a man who had just raped me for the second time not to tell anyone that he had raped me. One would think that if he ever called again, that I would report him for rape, now two rapes. But I believed a liar. I actually believed that he would not call me again like he promised. How gullible! Again, you would be correct. My still trying to "protect my parents' reputation" informed my decision. You would think I would tell them what the rapist had done at this point, right?

I received a call two weeks later. I cried and begged him to leave me alone. At the second rape, he had a gun in a holster, and laid it near my head. As he raped me again, I thought he would kill me and stop this torture of my body. Afterward, I went home and cried for the next two days. My parents had wondered about me and why I was upset. I couldn't tell them. By then, I had been raped twice. Repeatedly within the rapes themselves. So I thought they would blame me for those decisions to go to meet with him. I was a fourteen-year-old teenager, not in my right mind, and very afraid of that hate-filled man that he was going to kill me after I saw the gun.

Once more he called, once more I went and begged him not to rape me because of my monthly period. He said, "Prove it!" After lowering my pants, he threw me down and raped me once again. By this time, feeling like the fool I was, I resolved to tell someone. As I told you before, I had told my best friend Rebecca. That was the conversation we had had about the three rapes. She wanted me to tell my parents. Having remembered her words, I resolved to do so. She also said that my old boyfriend had bragged about how he and I had sex every time he came to see me. And that my reputation was considered bad because of that. I was livid hearing this. We dated for two years. And all this time people in that community where I lived thought that.

That next Saturday, I received another telephone call from that rapist. He began to tell me where to meet him. That's when I told him that I was going to tell my parents and report him for raping me three times to the police! He hung up the telephone immediately. I went to find my parents to report what he had done. Again, I was afraid. That was the reason I allowed the rapes. First, I didn't want my parents to know that I had disobeyed them by not coming home with the people I had been permitted by them to go with. Second, after I had been raped by this man so many times, I felt that their disgust would be even worse toward me. That they would blame me for the embarrassment to the family name.

But I also knew that these rapes had to stop. I called Rebecca and told her about the telephone call from this rapist. I also told her if anything should happen to me, or if I were shot with a gun, that she was to tell everyone everything I had told her about all the rapes and why I kept going back out of fear of being exposed to the town for being my fault in the beginning. I told her that I felt nothing during any of those rapes. If he expected me to join him in his experience, he found out each time he did this that that wasn't going to happen. I told my brother Pee-Wee that too. Nothing. There was nothing from me, no actions, no words, no encouragement that I was enjoying this rape, ever. Yet that didn't discourage this rapist not to return. My begging him to stop calling and being upset and crying just increased his determination. And after each encounter, my feelings of filth and shame returned.

It never occurred to me later that Rebecca had never condemned me. That she had never blamed me for going back those times, just to undergo further pain and suffering in those horrible moments of continuous pain and suffering. I was afraid not to. I still believed that he had the upper hand because he would tell my parents what had happened. How stupid of me now, right? As a fourteen-year-old immature girl, I didn't have the maturity to assess that I was the one with the upper hand, not that criminal. In those times of the rapes, I pretended to be somewhere else. I had to, to make what was happening go away. But it never did. Now, at that moment in my life, I was afraid to be alone at any time of the day. I felt worthless and cheapened, thinking I had something to do with it. I turned from being an innocent, free-flowing, effortless girl to a guilt-ridden and hateful individual. I had lost the one thing I had prided myself on, my virginity.

God is merciful and kind

Hell, in green pastures

This pain stayed with me, both physically and mentally. Now if anyone wanted to love me and ask for my hand in marriage, I would have to tell him why I no longer had my virginity. I would have to explain the entire crime to him. And I couldn't do that. He would think that I had done this on purpose and was lying, especially about the multiple rape occurrences. No, he wouldn't believe me. I dreaded getting married now. I never wanted to be touched by a man. I couldn't cross that barrier of feeling unworthy. I didn't deserve the love of a husband or anyone.

All those feelings took root in my mind, body, soul, and spirit. And I found that I needed help dealing with them. These feelings of listlessness stayed with me for decades. I experienced them even into my late twenties. And this emotional distress affected my dating, which I stopped doing right after the attacks. I couldn't trust a man not to harm me again. I group dated during this period. I felt safe in a group of friends. But now my friends were getting married or had begun dating others. I was left alone with my pain. I had never told them about the rape. Remember, I felt I wasn't worth anything anymore. The only comfort and safety I felt was at home. So, I stopped socializing at all. I stayed at home with my parents. Even they were surprised that I didn't go out any longer. But they accepted it after I told them that I was tired of going out, and just wanted to stay home. I did even through my late twenties. But the burden was getting harder, as even some of my siblings were wondering and asking why I "didn't date somebody."

Around this time, I decided to go to college. I had begun working at Broyhill furniture company, and this was nothing I wanted to do the rest of my life. Although members of my family had worked there, I didn't want that to be my final legacy. My mother had been taking me along with her as a travel companion on her Fourth of July week vacation to California. While there, I experienced something I had not experienced after the rape crime. That was freedom. I no longer felt unacceptable. In fact, I felt only joy and peace while in California. Unencumbered and unafraid. This was new to me, and I felt great.

Mama and I had gone there for vacations for years. At one point a group of family members took campers and drove there. On one of those trips I made a decision. A decision I knew would hurt the feelings of my parents and my siblings. I made a plan to move to California to live with my sister Mary.

My first attempt at moving there was good and lasted for the summer of 1970. However, I moved home to finish college because I had no skills with which to find meaningful employment. But in that period, just having been there for three months, I was certain I wanted to return to California.

Mary had moved there a decade earlier. She had become very successful, working for a vice president of a well-known bank. After a very emotional series of saying goodbye to family, friends, and other loved ones, I set out for San Diego to live with Mary. So, I began my time in San Diego, California. It was sheer freedom from emotional pain. And for a while, it worked.

One day, while attending a church, I decided to give my life to Jesus. Nothing rushed or pressured me to do that. I just wanted to be like the men and women I had grown up with, and whom I had admired all my life. For some reason, they were always loving and kind. Very sweet to me, and cared for me even as I had grown into an adult. My main examples were my mother and father, whom I had begun to have fun with as an adult. And yes, it had hurt them both tremendously that I left North Carolina. My mom later said that if she had known that would happen, she would have taken someone else with her. Wow, did that touch me! But now, I wanted that peace she and Daddy had—that atmosphere that had permeated our home all of our lives under Harve and Lucille Mayes's roof. And so, I accepted Jesus into my heart.

Perhaps my staying in Taylorsville, or for that matter anywhere in North Carolina, would have been or turned out better for me.

After all, I had been offered a job at a college in Boone North Carolina, so I could still move back there to Taylorsville and be closer to my parents. But by then my thinking had been clouded again by another controlling environment. One that only a church can inflict.

Biblical Legalism 101

I had been attending a denomination known for its legalistic teaching about the work of God. Their philosophy took the Bible and turned it into something to Jewish Hasidic culture. But instead of using the Torah, they used Bible scriptures. For example, if a scripture verse says women should dress with all modesty, their reading of that to their way of interpretation was dresses are to be below the knees, which excluded being seen at the beach in a bathing suit. You actually had to wear long pants to take a swim. Or if the scripture indicated that it is a sin to use color to make enhancements to your completion, their interpretation of that wording was not to wear any makeup, period. Likewise, with jewelry. Too much of that meant in their eyes that you as a woman were trying to draw attention to yourselves from the men in the congregation.

Notice that all these so-called "enhancements" of the word of God mainly applied to women in the congregation. As a woman, you were to place a cloth over your lap while sitting in the church so as to not tempt men in the pulpit or nearby. Oh, and the clincher, no wearing of open-toe shoes. This included sandals and high heels in the church. No short-sleeve dresses or low-cut dresses showing any part of your breast. No such regulations for men, however. They could pretty much do, wear, say, and act anyway they wanted to. No restrictions. I am not exaggerating in the least. These rules, similar to those in certain Muslim societies, still continue in some of these churches. And where they do, the pastors see no problem in these rules. This leaves women who leave the denomination not knowing where to land in normal church settings.

Women who stay can have emotional paranoia following a dress code that blames them for temptation that men "may" have in seeing them in makeup. Worst, women who are still there have to conform in an atmosphere of unfeeling and slavish regulations that pertain only to women in those congregations. The emotional imposition placed on young female children who are impressionable and are supposed to be discovering how their emotions and womanhood operate at that age are stifled. Can you also see how the distortion of the scriptures can lead to chronic misinterpretations of the rest of the Bible and its meanings to life in our time?

My experience mirrored the above, until one day I heard God's voice say to me, "I never told you that you had to remain here." This came after another contrived incident that the pastor thought he had seen. One night at choir rehearsal, the pastor showed up and indicated that I and another "sister" had switched places in the choir section. For some reason only known to him, he began a long countdown to zero, insisting that at the end of it that "whoever was out of their stations had better move back into their proper places." I can assure you that no one had any idea what he was talking about, and after the childish countdown from ten was over, he pointed to me and my good friend and said that we were on probation and couldn't return to the choir for a month.

Well, that was not punishment to us. Not having to stay for choir rehearsal all day Saturday to us meant we could go home after we helped clean the church. We were very happy about that. And we laughed while others stayed the entire day. But the second minister in charge saw our glee, and reported it to the pastor. When he found that his punishment in fact had brought us joy, he wouldn't have it. Oh no! The pastor couldn't have that, now could he? Someone being happy in his church after he had "punished" the two of us. Well, the joke was on him. After two weeks of this "punishment" and our checking off in the early afternoon got on his nerves, he made us return to the choir and made us sit in our "proper chairs." We had never left our proper seats in the choir the first time. We had been in those same places for as long as we had been in rehearsal over the years. But according to that pastor, not so. I know such antics seem childish, and they were childish. That evening the Lord God had a solution for me and her and her husband, although he didn't know it yet.

My friend told me that this was it for her, that she would not be returning. And she never did. In fact, she had her husband, a co-minister, made the excuse for her. Eventually she gave her husband an ultimatum. "We leave this town and move back with family, or you can stay here without me." The co-minister had a decision to make. He talked about staying there, because she, as a wife, needed to obey his rule. But when it came to the last Sunday night that they were told that they had better show up, neither of them did. That was the last time I saw either of them, and I thanked God for it. The co-minister had finally come to his senses.

That same evening at church services, I heard the Lord's voice clearer than I had ever heard. He spoke to me like someone would to a friend sitting nearby. The Lord told me every movement that the pastor would make. I heard God's voice say, "And next he will do this. And next he will say this." And he did. The Lord said, "Next, he'll come off the stage for effect, raising his voice louder." He did. Every time I heard God say what the pastor was about to do, the pastor did it exactly as God said he would do. I was truly amazed and astonished at what was being said by God and what the pastor did the very second in following Him. This went on as long as the service proceeded. Then I heard God tell me explicitly that I was not in any way, shape, or form to return to that church again. Having experienced God's voice, hearing Him speak, I was not in any way disobeying. I never returned to that church or any church in that denomination again.

God is restorer.

After leaving that church, I briefly attended others for a time being. I was without a church for a while, until I had a discussion with a friend named Linda. We both worked for the county of San Diego at the library headquarters. We both were library technicians. She and I became very close friends there, and both being Christians, our conversation went to this subject. Eventually she asked me if I attended a church. I then told her about what had happened to me at that COGIC church. She asked me to come with her to her church where she lived. The church was called Meridian Baptist. I said I would try. For me, that meant that I would have to make a half-hour drive to get there. But I wanted to try.

After I got there, I found the members to be welcoming and clearly liked my being there. Many walked up to greet me and shake my hand. I was in shock. I hadn't experienced that since I left my home in North Carolina. But I loved it. It made me feel human. It made me feel so warm inside. Not caution or fearful like I had felt at the other church environment. I didn't smile back too often, though. I needed to get over the shallowness that I had experienced before. Pretty soon I returned and made the church my home. I had found a place where I fit in. And the drive didn't seem long at all during this period of time.

Eventually I became involved in the church choir and began going to the Wednesday food fest and Bible teaching. Great food, great teaching. I was very happy there. I also was introduced to another of Linda's friends named Pat. She was in a wheelchair due to an illness, but she fully expected she would "escape it." She had faith that God would eventually heal her entire body. I agreed with her on that.

As time went by, I became stronger in my walk with God there. The pastor, Perry, was a fantastic pastor who loved the flock. He also had the gift of teaching. Phil, Pastor Perry's brother, also presided over the college aged as pastor. The choir director was Ron. Since I had been in the choir at my church in North Carolina, I decided to join the choir. I was welcomed and accepted with great love. The church offered two worship services. It had grown that much and more since Pastor Perry had been there. His teachings were with great authority and power and biblical: based in truth. Not read and then distorted like the legalistic church I had left behind.

As a choir member you were required to be there for both services, one at 8:30 and the other started at 10:45. We would sing at the first service and sit down to listen to the sermon. We then would sing for the next service. Afterwards some members would leave for home or other duties there. At times I did stay for the second service. I wanted to see and meet with my friends coming for one. We would see, greet, and then hug.

The reason I responded so well to this environment was it was true affection and the love of God shone on their faces. Two, there was order from the pulpit, not angry words that demeaned you for not living up to the philosophy practiced there like the former pastor did. In other words, if that pastor heard anything about you, he would berate you in front of the congregation, or on a Sunday morning take your "sin" to the pulpit and preach a sermon about it. That is what I mean by saying I didn't have to fear what or who was going to get grilled that day.

Many people had wisely left the former pastor's church prior to myself. They had seen through that man's false portrayal of God. We were under condemnation if we did or thought something that was considered a sin by that pastor. Nor did I have to worry about becoming something special to excite the audience to prove I was a believer. That was the reason I was at Meridian Baptist.

Another reason was that my friend had asked me to accompany her on a trip to San Francisco on a two-week vacation. She was doing the driving. She had brought along her little girl, age five. She was a doll, Miss Ava. When Linda and I talked on the phone, Ava would answer the call first. When she did, I began to ask her, in baby talk of course, what she was doing. Once, she mentioned that she had been playing with her stuffed rabbit. Well, this went on practically all the time. I would call, Ava would answer, and I talked to her in baby speak. One day I was in the car as she drove to work. I asked Linda about Ava. That was when she told me that Ava had asked her why I talked like a baby on the phone. Apparently, Ava had been talked by Linda to speak in regular tones. She, Ava, thought that was the way I spoke! In baby speak. I just died laughing! As the weeks wore on, I met her families in different parts of northern California: her father, Shep, her stepmother, Joan, and relatives from all sides.

It was a learning experience. For two weeks I was away from that legalistic congregation in San Diego. Those weeks away gave me clarity on how my life was going. In fact, I refer to that time in northern California as having my brain "deprogrammed." This was how I was able to leave that church. I had been away long enough to see the danger on the streets as a threat to me. I had to walk or ride a bus there. The type of housing changed from middle class to run-down homes there. One night I was walking to the former church and I walked straight into a gang of Crips and Bloods. Now the only reason I know that is that I had heard these whistled signals being sent out before I got to the church. These men had seen me walking many times.

At one point I stopped and made conversation with them after one asked me a question. They were nice to me, but I knew who they were. On my way back home, I noticed that the streets were quiet, no car traffic, no people walking around. Even the stores were closed. From this observation, I knew too that there would be a rumble, and I sped up to get home. On a neighborhood street surrounded by homes whose lights were all turned off and no one outside on the porches, I heard that whistle again. I was worried and began to look around, expecting that I was in trouble. Then I heard a sharp whistle. I turned around to see who it was when a man appeared on the street directly behind me. I looked at him, and he stared at me in menacing way. I stopped, and as I looked at him, he changed his look from menacing to disgust.

He said in frustration, "Oh! It's just that church lady!" With that, he turned away from me and disappeared behind one of the homes. I stood there, looking at him. I was scared out of my head. I practically ran home, praying for God's continued protection. I had to go down streets without lights and across a deserted field before I got to the place where I was staying. After that, I never walked to the church. I caught the bus.

This is what my friend Linda Kerr via God had saved me from. Thus, the trip to San Francisco turned me away from that place. I had been staying with some friends there. After that encounter and the incident with the Crips and Bloods, I moved away from that place and that church. Thus, the year without attending one. But now at Meridian Baptist under Pastor Perry Floyd's teaching, I was thriving. And the most important turning point in my life was that I began to hear the voice of God more. In fact, being able to discern God's voice so clearly was what got me out of the danger zone of that legalistic church. And I wanted more of that. And it began to happen. More and more each day. I attended Meridian for a year.

Unfortunately, my tenure there at Meridian was coming to a close. There was an eventual split among the members over whether to have choir music or a worship team. While I am sure that there was more to it than I wasn't privy to, members did have to make a choice whether to stay there or move on to a different place. What occurred was that the members who wanted to experience a different method of worship had to move to the new church. Those members who wanted to stay with the traditional setting remained at Meridian. This caused great concern and splits in families who had attended there for decades. But our prayer was that no bitterness would invade the hearts of members.

Meridian had been a place where the entire family attended together. Fathers, mothers, sons, and daughters attended there as one unit. That was one of the dear memories I had from there, and what I saw at Meridian. We had the same atmosphere at my church in our town of Taylorsville. Now that was not the same picture. Some turned their backs on those of us who had voted to move away. But over the years, God granted all of us time to come together at picnics to fellowship again as we once had.

I wrote a poem for Linda and David, her husband. We had many dinners together with other friends. That night at their house, she introduced me to artichokes. With butter! The entire evening was so wonderful. This is the poem:

Laughter the key;

Upon a stormy day, between the clouds,

streaks of sunshine opened a world of

Color and smells, so pungent!

Swirling leaves over and around, poking flowers and green trees holding a bouquet of cascading beauties,

Some tall, some small, some blunt edged, some red, some yellow, some white. The fruit of the garden delights, none unwelcomed in the early evening. As were visitors to this expanse of enticing beauty, slowly strolling around, and around and around in a circle complete.

Laughter as warm as the sun that ripens the berries growing around a fruit altogether different; flowing throughout the garden of peace and tranquility.

Mary, Mary quite contrary, how does your garden grow so green on St. Patty's day? Green artichokes, green grapes, green cake, green ice cream. A cook's green attempt, triumphed and tantalizing in its perfection.

She unbowed by the challenge, rose above the earth, to bloom in her success; and so shower such in her and his love for rooted and grounded friends.

Laughter, the key. Laughter, the results.

written for Linda and David, who gave us a special day)

Now Pastor Perry and his wife Kasey had planned to resign, which he did, as to, in his words, "not split the congregation." He said his farewell, as did his brother Phil as music director. Perry had plans to move back to Texas and live there. But what emerged was a group that desired a new worship aspect, and had asked him to stay. More than a few, who like me had decided to leave, were invited to a meeting with Pastor Perry and his wife. The meeting was called to see if Perry decided to stay, if he could support his family on the salary that Meridian offered him. As the pledges came in on amounts or tithing, the results were read off. The money pledged was thousands above what Meridian had paid him. After much prayer for a long period of time, Perry decided to stay.

We first met outside on Sundays at the park near a high school as we waited to find a place for the new congregation to stay. Over my begging to remain meeting in the park versus a building, Perry wisely said, "We have to move to this place in order to get out of the rain and wintertime." I looked stunned after he said this. Duh! Or eureka! Whichever you want to use here. Perry just smiled.

While at Grace, our new congregation, I became involved with the worship praise band. We had all the gifted people needed, and members filled the positions. I played the tambourine at first. I then graduated to being the conga player. One day the music director, Pastor Phil, just put them in front of me at rehearsal one night and said, "Here. Play these." I banged a little, but really had no knowledge of what I was doing. Now don't be angry with Phil. I found that to be an honor in that he knew I could play them with practice. However, I didn't expect that the congas would be set up and waiting for me when I arrived at church that following Sunday.

There I was, standing in front of an audience who was expecting me to bang away on them. And I did just that up there in front of the congregation: bang on them. At the end of services, I received compliments for what I had done. And they were glad for me and looking forward to hearing more. Now in addition to that trial by fire, Phil also asked me to lead a song, "Be Bold; Be Happy." Well I wasn't bold nor bold enough to sing. He insisted. After many rehearsals, the Sunday came that I had to sing at the "featured" artist moment. The good news is that I really belted the song out, which got a very enthusiastic response. Maybe because they were in shock that I sang, or liked the song I sang. Either way, it was a hit.

Also at Grace, I was appointed to be the coordinator over the newly formed singles' group. I had asked Pastor Perry if we could form one at church. I'd been attending a singles group at my friend Linda Kerr's house for Kehilat Ariel, and loved it. Imagine that, a social setting and I loved it. What a change in my soul. The fellowship was great, and we did fun things. So, after Perry gave his blessing, we began meeting. We did a lot of active activities and would meet at houses to have Bible studies during the opposite week, and an outing during the other weekend. As I had been designated the leader, I had to lead the studies. I remember being very intimidated by this, as I had never done that before. Ever! I prayed and asked God to please lead me in what to say, to act how to act, as I didn't know all of them personally. And again, I began to hear God's voice even more clearly. Just like He was in the next room.

I began to have prophetic dreams, not knowing how to handle what I had just dreamt. And yes, God kept talking to me about situations that would come up and how they were to be handled. I loved this. I shared with our group on how to hear God's voice better. One question was: How do you know it's Him speaking? That one was easy for me by now due to Perry's teachings and my own past church experience. I answered that you can tell the differences between God, yourself thinking, and Satan by knowing God's word, the Bible. Knowing how God speaks and knowing where God's heart is was all that was needed. I taught that if there was a direction that was given, and you were not sure how to turn or which way to go, just wait. Key word. Just wait. God doesn't rush you into anything. In fact, he has already in most cases spoken to you. Warned you what not to do but where to follow.

I also said to compare what you heard with what you know of God's character and characteristics. He never lies; he treats someone in the Bible who is in the same distress or issue just like you are in making decisions. And most importantly, give yourself time to ponder what the "voice" had said. God would never tell you to sin, or do this to yourself in his name, or that your God is strict and unloving, so pay no attention to Him. Or if He says He doesn't want you to succeed, not really! Those are examples of lies that Satan tells God's sons and daughters. And I do mean ALL of us. It's going down the road of "IF." With Eve, Satan used the tactic of "IF." "If you eat of this apple, surely you won't die." "IF" he loved you, he would allow you to eat anything in your garden. He's holding back on you, right?

Anything that Satan says is always untrue and planted to trip you up in life. To make you stumble and fall. To misdirect you, deceive you, to plant doubt in your mind to really confuse you and keep you asking God, "Why haven't you..." God wants the best for ALL his children on planet Earth. And yes, there is only one inhabited planet in the galaxy. Don't believe the Mormons and their talk about the "many planets" that they claim to operate and they have people living there already.

Nor will God rush you into making a decision. All things can be put off for a short or long time, giving you a moment in time to listen for His own true voice. King David did this after he had won a battle against their enemies: *The Philistines also came and spread themselves in the valley of Rephaim. 19 <u>And David enquired of the Lord, saying, Shall I go up to the Philistines? wilt thou deliver them into mine hand? And the Lord said unto David, go up: for I will doubtless deliver the Philistines into thine hand</u>* (2 Samuel 5:18-19).

On another occasion of the enemy attacking, David asked, "Shall we go up against?" God answered and told David "no." But it wasn't because He didn't want them to fight. He wanted to give the Israelites a new way of attacking them. The earlier tactic to defeat the Philistines wouldn't work for the next battle. He needed a new one to defeat his enemies. So, God told King David how to attack the enemy army. And David followed God's instructions. David defeated the enemy soldiers again, and defeated them all this time. David may have thought to fight the same way since the battle had been successfully won. But he listened to God and did win the battle again, thus routing the enemy from the hills.

1 Chronicles 14:13-14 King James Version (KJV)

[13] And the Philistines yet again spread themselves abroad in the valley.

^14 *Therefore David enquired again of God; and God said unto him, go not up after them; turn away from them, and come upon them over against the mulberry trees.*

The lesson for you and me is to listen patiently for the true voice of God. And then too, studying the word of God will point you in the right direction as to what you hear in "your ear." After learning this revelation, I too began to trust God and what He was telling me. Believe it or not, training yourself to listen to God and His way, and learning how He speaks is exceptional. Just like the community of Bereans. And the method God uses to help us to hear His voice? God calls it "homework." Do quiet times like King David did before going into battle. And like Jesus did when He went to pray on the mountaintop and returned by way of walking on top of the water. Alone time with God is crucial to your growth in Him. Hearing His instructions, David won the two battles.

Now just remember. There is not pass or fail here. We all at some point fail and mistake God's voice as the enemy. This is why the quicker you learn from God and how He operates, the easier hearing becomes. Just remember, slow down to make decisions when possible, no matter the circumstances. And ask God immediately for guidance. And if you can wait, do wait. God will bring the solution either very quickly or later with the appropriate answer for the situation you are facing.

Unfortunately for me, I didn't realize just how much stress I was under doing both church work and work at my job. During this time in my life, I had a tiny stroke. A TIA. The stroke occurred while I was at my desk at work. I fell asleep, which I never did, and was out for a while. My library director came to the door and called my name. Apparently, other staff had tried to and couldn't get me awake, and panicked. I thought I was okay. Just sleeping, I told her. What really had happened was that I had passed out. Then later as I drove home and was getting out of the car, I became very dizzy. I staggered about like someone who was drunk. I tried to steady myself. I was determined to pick up the balloons for a work party the next day. I drove home very carefully, as my home was a short distance away, thank God. I could barely climb the stairs to my bedroom. I had trouble moving my left leg. I stumbled into my bed and stayed there until Mary came home.

I slept from that time on to the morning. Mary kept calling me to get up to go to work. I couldn't. After I told her what had happened and my symptoms, she insisted I call the doctor. It had been almost a week since the incident at work. By now my arm had become plastered in one position on my side, and I couldn't move it from that position. Also, my leg had drawn up, which left me limping. She did get me to my doctor. After his examination, he told me that I had become a victim of a stroke, and sent me to a neurologist. I was in shock at his diagnosis, as was Mary, who became deeply concerned over another one happening. I had sick leave, and I told my boss my condition. I went to see the neurologist, and he examined me to see why the stroke had happened. What he said was extraordinary.

He found where the stroke had occurred. It was in the right inside lobe of my ear. He also said that I was lucky they'd found it, as it was a rare case in strokes. He also said that he had recently read in the *New England Journal of Medicine* where a research doctor had written a report about these kinds of rare strokes. He said that the reason for mine was due to stress. That was why my left side was affected and my speech, as I couldn't form sentences anymore. Eureka!

I was absent from work for a while longer, and the paralyzing effect wouldn't leave on the left side of my body. But later on, when I went to church on Sunday, they all prayed for me to be healed. I believe those prayers were why I did heal over time. Finally, after a while, I could talk in full sentences. Then after that, I could feel the numb sensation leaving parts of my body on the left side. I had hope for full healing over time now. The next thing that happened was my arm and leg went back to their normal position. Hallelujah!!! Praise the wonderful name of God MY HEALER!! Grace celebrated too.

I had insisted on playing with the worship team as I had done before. And I did. Once. Before the healing began, people in the church and my close friends who knew me and knew what had happened rejoiced with me, seeing the miracle of God worked before them. But prior concerns were for my well-being in not doing too much, given my situation. So, I had to relinquish some of my duties and going to meetings during the week, which I loved doing and being there helping people. But now I had to take a look at my own situation and learn that I couldn't be there all the time. I also learned to take time out, like I said before, and study. To sit before God and learn how He speaks, how He teaches and taught, and how to alert myself to His voice if he wanted to speak with me. This is what I learned during this crisis in my life. And it wasn't pretty, and the crisis didn't feel good. So, I learned to wait on God, as He had taught David to do in his crisis with his enemies of Israel.

The enemy loves to take advantage of us as we walk with the Lord on a daily basis. The enemy's motive is not pure, nor are the ways of the enemy good. Our enemy Satan and the demons are truly out to harm us and make our lives as miserable as possible. So, I let that get to me. But not anymore. I learned the lesson. Treat God well, and with respect. He'll guide us through anything that may come our way and will give us the victory over it. Just like He did David, God will teach us to live in Him. With Him. And by Him. He'll teach us to walk with Him, by His side. Not our own gig. He lectures us to be kind to others, and pay respect to our elders. That is what I loved doing at this church and other churches I attended, as I had done that at Macedonia church in my hometown. So, let's believe

God is available at all times in our lives. And available to talk and speak with us. He makes our lives brand new!

God is Healer.

As I learned more about God and myself, I heard God speaking to me concerning some issues I had to confront in my life. Issues I had been running from since that terrible crime of rape had occurred. You see, Perry taught that God wanted all his sons and daughters to be healthy both inside and out. Healthy in how we cared for our bodies, and healthy in our innermost being. To that end Perry would preach and teach about removing those issues in our lives that were hindering our progress with God. And he based it on the disciples turning into Apostles as they got to know God better before and after his resurrection from the grave. Even Elisha developed into an experienced Prophet of God after being taught by his mentor Elijah. This is when Perry set up sessions just for those in our congregation to see a psychologist. Her name was Beverly.

Our sessions with Beverly began as one session of all of us meeting and talking about issues that might be useful to disengage from them in our lives. Those included domestic abuse, partners who were not believers and how to cope with that, alcoholism, drug abuse, miscarriages, child abuse, and, of course, rape.

She gave us a book to read on these subjects. She told us to write down anything that came up in our spirits, that made us become emotional, or resulted in painful memories that had occurred in our past or were developing in current lives that we were struggling with. After reading the book, I came to realize that I had never forgiven the man who had raped me on multiple occasions. I also realized at that moment that I had no intentions to either. He certainly didn't deserve it, in that he knew what he did was criminal, hurting and harming me and my body. Out of lust and hate, he had attacked numerous women. All I wanted was to see him burn in hell and punished beyond compare in the deepest and darkens corners of it. He deserved no less for the lives he had destroyed while he stood on God's earth, including my own. But I would have to begin the process of forgiveness in order to remove the poison he had deposited in my inner being both physically and literally.

At Grace, I was given more responsibility. This was prior to the stroke. One was being selected a co-leader of a home group that met in El Cajon, California. The other senior co-leader was Pat, the one who attended Meridian with me. We had continued our friendship, and it had grown over the years. She had decided to leave Meridian too, but a little later than the first group. She had not gotten the okay from God in her prayers to go with the first bunch. And she waited in obedience. That was the perfect way of doing such a move. After all, she had been in leadership at Meridian, and was well loved by practically everyone who attended there, especially those who had worked with her.

Just a note here that although some had decided to leave there, some did decide to attend other churches altogether different from either church. But one thing that more than a few of us as majority had decided to do was to keep the love of God toward each other no matter where we ended up. That did happen. We had a big reunion a decade later at Meridian. I missed it, but was told that I had been missed, people wanting to know why I hadn't come. That's what God had done for the old and new congregation. Families had reunited in part over the years. Friendships returned. Hurt feelings were healed on a personal way by God. Why? Because He saw that our hearts wanted that to happen, and so it did.

And as we all grew more into what our calling or destiny was and performed them for Him, more gifting immerged. That was Perry's teaching: allow God to set the time and place of his choosing to allow for your gifts to become operable. Whatever or wherever your heart led, this in most cases was a part of your destiny in the Messiah. "Your gift will make room for you," he often said to the congregation. There is where you will thrive. You and others around you will feel that and benefit from it. Do what you love doing whether being a school teacher, a manager of a company, a hairdresser, a nurse or doctor, or a low-paid skill set; do this in remembrance of God. And do it as if God was your employer, which He is. Do all to glory of God. My major gifting has happened to be a musician, teacher, counselor, and, for me, well...I'd find out my gifting would more than even I could imagine.

The gifts I had been using at Grace began to grow. God has a great sense of humor. One is that I am, in reality, shy. I never liked being in the front of an audience. I hated to be put on as the lead on anything. So, you can imagine my feelings when, while at Meridian and Grace, God placed me in front to be an extrovert. Not easy, but

God got me through it, and He was not finished with audiences. An introvert at heart, now I had to learn to convert to an extrovert.

As my healing evolved with the psychologist, I began to put the Word of God and the issues I had to off-load as baggage on God's altar. As I offered them up as a "fat" offering to allow God to burn them up, then He would take them up as an offering to him. And for me, He was just getting started.

I began the private interview with Beverly, for a more in-depth session. After her teaching and Perry's wisdom, I soon began to come to a point of dealing with the crime of rape. Perry had always said that rape is a crime, not sex. And if the police or newspaper said it was sex, it was sadly mistaken and had totally mispresented what had occurred. Rape is a crime, not having sex. Let me repeat that for those who would question that. Rape is a crime, not sex. And don't use the word "assault," which can and does have many correlations that don't always include rape in all its ugliness.

Sex, which I believe is made for the marriage bed, is when both partners have a personal sexual encounter with each other. Even the Navy has that wording or designation in delineating the difference. And they take it very seriously if anyone, military or civilian, doesn't agree with that meaning. Just ask those who have lost their jobs or command when they raped someone. And the Navy also teaches that it goes both ways. The Navy has recorded situations of even women in the higher ranks forcing men, and other women, using workplace threats, to force them to comply. And as usual, I'm afraid, men who are blackmailed and raped rarely report the crime because of fear of retribution if the complaint is acted upon. Maybe this one act that hardly gets press is when some male superior forces a lower-ranking male officer, using their rank and promotion if they don't comply, into rape. That being said, rape is considered a crime under any circumstance. Now it was time for me to come to grips with what had happened. I had never told anyone other than my best friend Rebecca. Now I had decided it was time to tell others. I began with Beverly Nelson.

I didn't think it would ever come out. I stuttered at first, but then there was no going back for me. I didn't think I could say the words, "I was raped as a young teenager." Immediately I felt shame, anger, confusion, vulnerable, filthy just like I had felt after the first rape. I felt sick to my stomach, and I cried. Oh, how I cried. Now the inner healing would begin, I hoped. I can't say how the session progressed after that one. But since I had uttered those words, my life seemingly took a turn. A good turn.

Over the course of counseling, Beverly probed and encouraged. She made it clear that the rapes, no matter how many, were a crime. Not of passion, but by a brutal, ugly, barbaric, unfeeling monster. A person who knew what they were doing throughout every step of the way, and there was absolutely no excuse for that crime, nor any justification possible. She said, "Rape is a crime that has a victim. That leaves that victim broken and crushed in spirit, body, and soul." Much damage is done to the psyche of that victim, as it did mine. I was never able to get my mind around a despicable, depraved, sickening mind that would do something so horrible to another human being. Something so heinous that people unknowingly recoil automatically when its mentioned. That is, unless you are a rapist.

The pain and agony of just going through an assault on your body in that manner is unbearable at times. And yes, my virginity being destroyed by a criminal who pushed my legs up over my head and I could do nothing to stop him but scream. And I certainly did. I actually struggled to get away and almost got loose. That is when he began to choke me. I almost passed out. Oh, I screamed at the top of my lungs prior to that. I knew someone had to have heard them. But no one came to my rescue. And oh, the pain during and after that violent rape. Indescribable. Yet I did have to describe it to

Beverly. And with that, the healing process of my body began in earnest.

God is peace.

In this day and age, what I felt after the rapes would be referred to as PTSD, Post-Traumatic Stress Disorder. After reading the symptoms listed, I can see how my actions before and after the rapes over a sustained period of time resulted in the PTSD. Also, Beverly walked me through these same symptoms, although not a concept then in practice, in allowing me to deal with each one. I recognized mine as depression, misery, despair, feelings of helplessness, guilt, sadness, worthlessness, anger for no reason usually directed toward my parents and anyone I once considered a close friend, not able to trust others even though a friendship existed, and mood swings. I carried these feelings and ideas inside for a period of almost twenty-five years of my life. Day after day I lived trapped in a miserable void. My body adapted to these feelings. At some point, they became unrecognizable. They had receded into the back of my mind so deeply, even I didn't recognize them as being there over a period of time. One can imagine having to come to terms with this imbedded turmoil raging inside your body.

I will list the symptoms for you:

Class 1 symptoms: The sufferer re-experiences the traumatic incident. *Examples:*
nightmares, flashbacks

Class 2 symptoms: The sufferer displays avoidance, wants to stay away from anything that may possibly remind her/him of the trauma. May also display lack of responsiveness or interest to all life circumstances. *Examples: sights, smells, sounds, conversations associated or reminding of trauma, unable to enjoy once joyful activities or have loving feelings*

Class 3 symptoms: Hyperarousal. *Examples: irritable all the time or inability to sleep* Read more: http://depressiond.org/ptsd-symptoms/

I came to the point of admitting to a psychologist what had happened to me. Why I was unable to form meaningful relationships with male friends. Why I didn't trust men no matter how I tried. That I would leave a room at the possibility of being in the same room alone with them. It wasn't their fault. That was the fault of a dark, depraved, cold animal, a heathen, who preyed on innocent women. A person who was a coward and sought out women in an attempt to gain control over them. A control freak. A freak, period. Believe me, I have many more names I could say.

He was not innocent; I was!!! I was the innocent party here. That nurse was the innocent party there in that hospital when he raped her. And every woman he had raped or had tried to rape and they got away, as I am certain there were other female victims, were ALL INNOCENT. And ANY person who has been raped from now on and into the future ARE INNOCENT TOO! The problem isn't the victim. The problem is with the terrorist rapists who get their kicks from demeaning and controlling another person.

Let me assure whoever is reading this book, if you are a rapist, YOU ARE THE CRIMINAL! And you will be found out eventually. And YOU WILL PAY for the crime. You will be the one who will suffer in prison, not those victims like myself that allowed my soul, heart, and body to impose a prison sentence on myself for what I thought. And did for far too long. The only thing I failed at was thinking my parents would lose their reputations, and that they would be ashamed at what I had allowed to happen after the initial rape episode. But nothing could have been further from the truth. I wrote a letter to them, confessing what had happened and what my thoughts were at the time in making those initial decisions, and to please tell my siblings what had occurred.

God is forgiving

I decided to write that letter, as I didn't think I could get it out verbally without crying. I was living in California at this time in my life. I didn't quite know what would happen or what they would do. But I do remember what I felt after I had written it. Pure release. Pure joy, for-real joy. God's joy, the joy in my spirit and in the very deepest of my soul joy. I was happy, really happy in my soul. I had been told that I was not the guilty party. On the contrary. The wrong done to me had no more to do with my actions than a train hitting an empty car stalled on the railroad. The engineer isn't the guilty party, and had done nothing to attract or draw the car's attention. But the jolt of hitting a car on the railroad affects more than the driver of the car. It leaves a lasting impression on the engineer and everyone seated on the train. Little did I imagine or realize the impact of news upon the rest of my family. They all couldn't have been more sympathetic, encouraging, loving, caring, and, yes, angry. But not angry at me. Their anger was directed at the rapist.

I received calls from each one of my brothers and sisters, and my mom and dad. I must say that I didn't expect such reactions. To be honest, I had actually forgotten that I had mailed it to my parents' home. I had finished the therapy so successfully, that my mind, soul, and body had moved into a new phase. A new season. But, remember the train wreck that I once was? Well, the passengers on the train had just felt the jolt, the impact from the train hitting the car of the irresponsible driver who had left their car on the track. Now my family had read the news. Finally. It was out now. Finally, and everyone knew.

I didn't know what to say.

Each called separately and could hardly speak. My brothers were very angry. My sisters had no words. Speechless. My brothers' anger boiled over, "...if I ever see him again..." "He'd better not show where I can see him." Much worse, but you can get the idea. "He took a gun to shoot you!" I could hear the sadness and anger in all their voices. Of just what I had to put up with for decades. "I can't see anyone doing this to you. You never did anything to anybody!" On and on. My dad and Mama said how hard it was for them to read it. They had to stop a few times. More than a few times. I believe the most, if there could be considered the most, egregious part of all was when I said in the letter, "he used my body for a hole over and over again. Multiple rapes at one time, over and over and over and over again."

They consoled me; I consoled them, my family. As adults we got along just great. We covered each other's backs. We took up for each other when one was attacked. We had learned to be honest among ourselves, as Mama and Daddy had taught us, and with others. No fighting in the house. No lies! We were taught it was better to tell the truth as the outcome was greater. The "hickory switch" or the leather belt was applied, if needed, for the more serious stuff. We as siblings tried not to let it get to that point. Because those instruments of punishment hurt sometimes. But as a teenager, being grounded for two or three weeks seemed to hurt the most.

I remember once when seeing my friends and spending time with our group dates became too much physically and I needed to sleep. I actually asked my parents to ground me so I could rest. I didn't want to lie to my buddies, as I had no reason not to join them at events. You should have seen the expressions on their faces. Daddy actually laughed. I told them why, and so they complied. I got two weeks off from social events and got some needed rest. We loved and respected each other. We cared for each other. That was the way it was and is to this day.

I wish I had trusted that more. But as a young new teenager, you think that "you know best." I really wanted to tell Mama and Daddy. And I also think that my not telling them about the rape hurt them. I shared everything with them normally, and we talked openly and often about things all the time. But I thought they would be angry with me for that, and for breaking the rule they set of coming back with those that they had approved. I was the one who didn't follow their very exact instructions, which put me in the path of a rapist. Had I told them the truth, I would have received comfort, care, and love. Just like I did when I told them decades later. Like the prodigal son's father, Mama and Daddy would have rushed to embrace me had I told them earlier. Both did when they learned my tragic secret. Again, many lives had been affected horribly with the sad news in that letter. But in that letter, I told them about Dr. Beverly and the work she had done with me, getting me past the rough part of the ordeal. With the bad news, I could tell them how good I felt about myself. Feeling whole and my well-being. That by God's grace and patience, I had begun the long process of healing and forgiveness.

God's justice flows in when we least expect it.

One of my brothers, Pee-Wee, called me to tell me that the rapist had left the town and was in a neighboring city. I didn't realize until later in the conversation that the reason he knew that was that they were always on the lookout for him. Needless to say, I told him that it was good that they hadn't. I told my brothers that the rapist wasn't worth their spending time in jail for a crime.

But the rapist soon returned to the area. Pee-Wee, who had come to pick me up at the airport, told me about the encounter.

By chance, he saw him in a parking lot at the Red Lion Supermarket in their town. He saw him walking toward the supermarket. My Pee-Wee went right up to him and said, "You raped my sister." He said the rapist didn't say a word but turned around and headed back for his car. My brother continued to follow him to his car, saying, "She told all of us about it. How would you like it if someone raped your relative? But they wouldn't have to, because she puts it out there for any and every man she comes across." By this time, the rapist had reached his car having never responded to my brother's comments. My brother called him a few more names like coward and made more comments. "Why you walking away?" By this time, the rapist reached his car and got in with my brother still talking in tow.

My brother said he "high-tailed it out of there" scared. I looked at my brother. I could only look, because the emotions for what he had done for me was overwhelming. I could only smile at Pee-Wee and say "thank you." My brother took up for me. My brother confronted the rapist. Had the rapist not moved on or challenged him in any way, Pee-Wee would have had reason to give him the beating that the rapist's parents missed giving him while growing up.

And there's more.

I arrived at home and greeted my mom and dad with a big hug. I was on a trip for my employer and had swung by for a few days. I visited with family and friends, and looked forward to seeing others. I looked forward to seeing my church moms as well. Aunt Emma was one I always tried to see. I looked forward to seeing Aunt Sarah too at church. I got there just for the preaching session. I didn't go to the Sunday school for adults.

As it so happened, when I entered the church, I sat down at my "usual" seat located midway up the row and next to a window. I loved that window on "that side" of the building. Daddy had placed stained glass window treatments on all the windows. They were beautiful, and I had told him so. My mom was in the choir section. It was the adults' turn to sing for the service that Sunday. I noticed her up there and waved. She had a strange look on her face, though. I couldn't read it. She looked agitated and was moving uncomfortably, squirming in her seat. She nodded her head for me to look to my left. And I saw him, the rapist. He was sitting with his family.

There is a long southern tradition in the smaller churches where visitors and retuning members like me were to say a few words at the special time in the service in which to speak. The pastor at that time, Clowning, had just asked me to speak. I stood and said, "To Pastor Clowning, Deacon Board, officers of the church, church members, and my family." I spoke of how happy I was to be home again. That I looked forward to seeing the rest of my family and friends while there. This greeting is used by churches still to this day. It's a courtesy to address the senior serving-level group in such a way.

After I said that, I sat down. I was across on the other side of the church, but a few rows back. I could see the rapist. He had his back to me. He turned his head slightly to look at me. I saw that out of the corner of my eye. I did not return the look. I sat stoic, looking at the leaders in the pulpit. I did look at my mother, who was having a very hard time by now keeping her emotions under control. She still had that look on her face, but by then I knew why. The rapist had started coming to the church recently with his mother and father. This had really vexed my mother and my brothers.

As the service continued, I sat stoically, still looking ahead. Surprisingly, I had no reaction to seeing him. At least not one that was fearful. In fact, I felt no fear or trepidation, nor was I nervous at seeing him. Then I heard Jesus say, "You ARE healed!" This was when I knew how much I had healed on the inside. While glancing at my mother again, I saw the rapist glance at me again. This time, I turned and looked directly at him. The look on my face spoke volumes. But I doubt he knew what thoughts were running through my mind at that very moment. He didn't know me. Not at all. In fact, he would never know about the peace in my soul. He would never see me scared again as long as he lived on the earth. I had no fear of him, and that much he could see from my face.

Running through my head were the words "You thought no one would ever know, didn't you? You thought I would never tell anybody, didn't you? You thought you had gotten away with it, didn't you?! Now who's running scared? Now who has fear in their soul? Now it's you shaking in your boots. Where is your gun now you...?" That's why he turned away so abruptly. The coward that he was until the day he died. Oh yeah, years later when I heard he was sick and, on his deathbed, I said then, "You won't be smirking at God now. He's going to wipe that grin right off your face. And I have no sympathy for you. In fact, I could care less about your death. I hope God puts you in the deepest, darkest part of hell where all the things you did to me and other women you raped will happen to you there. That you are raped repeatedly eternally."

When I looked back and saw my mom again, she was smiling. She witnessed the stare-down I gave him. He was the scared one now. She obviously didn't know what my thoughts were. But she knew me well enough to know, from my expression and mannerisms, that I had NO FEAR of him now. NO fear!

After service let out, the members wanted to greet me. Normally that is so wonderful, to get hugs, the "How are you?" The smiles from my cousins and their asking me what are you doin' out there in California now? But I don't think they understood my countenance right then. And I could see their disappointment, so I slowed down and talked. After all, I had only one Sunday. After that I would be leaving. As soon as I could greet them, I literally ran outside to confront the rapist. But before I could reach the parking lot, his parents greeted me. I tried to act respectfully as I could toward them given the circumstance. They too were happy to see me, as was their daughter. Since I had visited their home regularly, I understood that. After all, we had been friends once. After a few words, they asked if I would come by the house before I left for California. In shock, I merely said that I would try. After a while, I said my goodbyes to them. I turned around to see if I could locate the rapist, their son, again.

I spotted him in the parking lot. He was in conversation with a group of girls. As I strolled toward him, my progress was interrupted by another church member. A senior church member. I had to arrest my speed to chat with her. It would have been impolite and insulting had I not. We spoke for a while. I told her how living in California was just okay sometimes, and mostly not with a few things that bothered me. We finished our chat.

I turned to move forward to the rapist. He never saw me coming up behind him. I could not believe my eyes. He was talking, the only male, to this group of teenage girls. He was trying to flirt with them. I didn't have to imagine what he was saying to them. I could see by their expressions that these girls had no clue that he wanted to lure one of them away for a future encounter to rape one of them too. Their expressions were of girls who were enjoying a compliment from a man about their looks. I could tell that exactly by the way he approached them. Now I had to figure out how I could get to him. To get him away from the girls who were innocent and had no idea who or what he was.

One of my cousins tapped me on my shoulder and came in for a big hug. It was my close cousin, another one who attended the church. When our conversation was finally over, I turned to walk toward the group and the rapist again. But he was gone. My heart sank. The expression on my face at that moment perplexed my cousin, who looked at me puzzledly. I hadn't realized just how anxious I had become. I wanted to confront him. I wanted to look him in his face and tell him that he had been exposed. I am certain that I would have looked directly at him and said some other comments.

At that moment I was determined to allow others to know what he had done. During those multiple rapes, I refused to look at his face out of shame. I was in a horrible state of mind. No words. I looked around the parking lot to see if I could spot him. He was gone. Turning to find other friends, my intent was to tell the pastor what I saw. And also determined that I wouldn't allow him to get away with raping those young teenagers. I was once like them at that age. Just learning about my body. Enjoying how beautiful I was and looked. My brothers had told me that too. It also made them more protective. They admonished me about being careful and keeping my curfew. Well, I lost where these girls were now. I couldn't remember having that much freedom of thought and a carefree innocence. I still remembered that scene. After a rape, continuous rapes, even if someone's healing has taken place, there is a part of your mind that will replay some of those scenes. The pain had lessened to almost nonexistence. But just so many things can suddenly trigger painful memories. PTSD.

After Mama and I arrived home, I talked to her about what had transpired. She agreed with me that he, the pastor, did need to be told. But I couldn't wait till next Sunday came around again as I would be leaving prior to that. So, we called him.

Mama made the call. After greeting him and going through all the expected southern traditions afforded the pastor of any church in the black community, she gave the phone to me. She said that "my daughter from California wants to speak with you, Pastor Clowning."

My mom watched as I launched into the story of the rape and the rapist with her pastor. He was quiet as I spoke. I told him about the way the rapist had fooled me and got me into a house so I could make a phone call. How he then proceeded to rape me. And as I told him more about the other rapes in the back woods of our house, my voice was firm and strong. No trembling. No hesitation. No halting speech. Just as I had told about the rape to many in San Diego, California, including my Pastor Perry. That I communicated clearly and firmly too. At the end of our conversation, Pastor Clowning asked one question or made a statement that suggested how some people in that area would have reacted had I told my story to a jury. The very same town where the nurse told the officials about how a serial rapist had raped her and made a charge of rape against him.

This pastor said, "Now you say he raped you multiple times. I kinda wonder since he raped you three times, if that was a rape."

My mother was watching me intently the entire time. Her eyes never left my face while I spoke to her pastor. My thoughts were: Why did I expect anything more in this place? And in my sadness, I felt that my feelings were mirroring her's perhaps at that moment when nobody believed her story either. They hounded her, that nurse who reported the rape, in that town. The serial rapist's parents and others in that town had said she had lied. That their son had not raped her. The police had held that rapist in the jail cell up town until a preliminary trial could be held. I too was one of those people who said that he could not have raped her. I remember that to this day. I had been at their house that weekend, and had heard them talk about her, saying that the only reason she said he had raped her was because she was white. That she was trying to blame the rape him because he was black.

Now the rapist had been in the hospital overnight, being treated for some ailment I didn't know of and was never told of by the family. The first day I saw him at the parents' house was the day he had been released from jail and the charges had been dropped. Well in my mind, that vindicated him. I told him that by saying it indirectly to those in the house. He was polishing his shoes, as he was going out on a date or something. To this day, I can't believe how gullible and naive I was. How stupid. But at that time, he had done nothing to me. He listened to me with disinterest, but kept staring at me, not saying a word.

I still believe to this day that his father had twisted the arms of some town officials to get his son out of jail. The town gossip was that he had raked her rape charge over the coals. The son was not prosecuted and was allowed to go free. I don't know if he got any probation. But his attitude was, "I can do anything and not be punished." I saw that in his manner and attitude. The stress of the experience made it so that the nurse couldn't even go out in public for a while, as her charge of rape claim had not been upheld.

Now I admire her courage. That incident was on my mind too, because I was the next victim of a brazen assault on me the next week. I'll never forget what I had said about the nurse not being truthfully, but for one main reason. A fact that was not lost on me as I explained before. If I had told anyone or the police about the first rape, people in that town would not have defended me either. In fact, from my reactions to the charge of the rapist, and some of those in my town, I knew this to be true. I was ashamed and demoralized. No one would believe me, I surmised after the raping. No one. I had failed in many ways. Lacked the courage. And this one came back to haunt me at that moment.

She, the nurse, was right. Perhaps the town people would have supported me had I given the evidence to the police that night. After all, my parents were well known by the community and greatly respected. Perhaps my ending would have been different from the nurse's situation, not ending in shame for me at all. Perhaps. Just perhaps. Then too, her charge would have been validated by my charge of rape. Yet, I didn't.

I hope you don't make the same mistake. Perhaps now, this will help the situation of someone you love who has been raped. Had I followed through and told the police what had happened, the rapist would have been taken off the street. And my outcome in life would have greatly changed. Even though I wished to this day that I had, eventually I did receive healing from God, and I've been healed. I hope and pray that she has too.

Had I told the police, the rapist would have been in jail for years. He raped her, he raped me, and I would suspect others. He never stopped. A serial rapist never does. The power of intimidation and control rules their lives. Couple with other issues of dominance, their kick is to make others suffer. Just as my letter broke throughout the extended family, one of my brothers told me that the serial rapist had tried to rape my cousin too. But she got away. See? My rape also released others to talk about the things done by the criminal. Getting back to my mother's pastor...

I began to weep when he said those words to me. "Well it may not have been a rape because it happened so many times." I lost it. Pastor or not, and unfortunately as a leader and pastor in that community, he didn't believe me. Now, I know that I lived in California. He didn't know of my reputation or of my ministry work in my church. Or that even if I was a believer. That said, his words were devastating and cut me to my soul. Indeed, my heart. I shouted at him that I was NOT lying! That I had told everyone in my family what had happened to me! That I had told my parents and they believed me! I said that my pastor at my church in California and many members knew! I shouted more. I said that the criminal did rape me! That he had threatened to tell this. At my younger age I couldn't think that through. I was still shouting and very angry and upset. How DARE you say that to me?! You have no idea what destruction this has brought me and my entire family! My mom or I having to sit in the audience at Macedonia or look from the choir stand, KNOWING THAT HE HAD RAPED ME. Looking at his face, KNOWING WHAT HE REALLY STOOD FOR AND HAD SHOWN NO OUTWARD CHANGE OF HEART FOR ANYONE! I said that he or I could tell ANYONE IN HIS CHURCH THAT HE HAD RAPED ME. I'm just letting you know that he was talking to those young teenagers in the parking lot. They think he is flattering them. But you have to stop him before he fools another one and rapes her.

The pastor then interrupted me and offered an apology, I believed a heartfelt one. I calmed down and looked at my mother. I had seen her moving uncomfortably in her favorite recliner as I yelled at the pastor. Not uncomfortable for what I was saying. But angry at the pastor for not believing me, and that he had made me cry. Her mouth was tight with biting words. But she allowed me to continue, still watching more intensely now.

Then the pastor said something shocking. I had calmed down after he apologized and said, "Now..." Then he said that he believed me. The pastor had obviously heard of other incidents of rapes by others by this man. He said that "he came into church one Sunday and had gone to the front to ask to join the church." Now I was the one listening intensely. He went on to say that "I allowed him to come in, but I didn't believe him when he said he had repented of his sins." He told me how his actions had not changed afterward, and that he was worried about his being there too, especially seeing him around the teenagers.

I told him that he had to watch him like hawk and reminded him that I had seen him in the parking lot talking to those young girls. That I was a young teen when I was fooled by that man with lies. I said that I thought I could trust him, as I was always over at their house visiting on Saturdays with his sister, my friend. After we ended our conversation, I hung up.

My mother still had that look on her face, which I had seen so many times growing up when she had become angry. She wanted to say much more during that conversation with Pastor Clowning but held her tongue. I love my mother and dad so much. They taught us so much in how to act and so forth. I turned to her and told her his exact words he had said. In those times there was no way to listen to a conversation unless you were on the other phone in the house in another room. We talked further and as she spoke, I calmed down too. She spoke gently to me, soothingly like she had always done. I finally stopped crying.

I had to leave to return to California. Later, after I got home and had moved on from the emotional trauma of the scenes from my hometown, I received a call from my mother. Time had slipped by as I move back into my ministries back in El Cajon where my church was. I had a conference with my Pastor Perry and told him what I had encountered in my trip home. I mostly concentrated on the exchange of comments with the pastor there about my rape experience. I explained how difficult it was, not for me, but for my family because the criminal had begun to attend. That seeing him there practically every Sunday was no joy for them. I say this because that is what my siblings had told me about their reactions to his being there in the congregation.

My brothers and sisters have always been involved in the running of the church as leaders and as supporters to the various pastors who came and went for decades. Especially Bettye, the eldest. She led a vacation Bible school that was held during the week. This practice too went on for decades. I taught classes there during the week of Bible school too. I was in the church choir at the age of nine, after which it turned into an adult choir. I barely got in that one because I was so young, but I made it. All my siblings were in the choir at one time or another. When our sister Bettye left to attend her husband's church in Statesville, the first thing she did was to take a leadership position working as a volunteer, and yes, singing in their church choir as well.

I relayed the words I said to the pastor in in my hometown, and his response to me. Perry allowed me to speak for quite some time. I was very happy that I had or had attempted to confront the rapist right then and there. But he had escaped me. I know he saw me inching closer to him, and so he fled. I know it! I saw the fear in his face the second time he turned around to look at me. He was VERY afraid. He knew that I had told my family, and that one of them had tried to get him to do anything, say anything, so that they would have the excuse to beat him up. Right then and there in that parking lot. And that I wanted to do the very same thing. But with talking **out loud** in that church parking lot for ALL to hear and to witness my words.

Perhaps that opportunity would present itself again. But it did not. And now I know why. I had spent years trying to get through this intense emotion to confront the man who had mauled me and assaulted me, using my fear and age at that time to intimidate me. I used my knowledge of my belief in Jesus Christ to lead me during those years of healing—emotionally, physically, and mentally. I had put on weight that amounted to over three hundred pounds. In fact, that was the very thought that came to my mind sitting in that congregation as he turned to look at me. I had put on weight to make me ugly to men. Any man. At any time. Because if I was as beautiful as I once was when I was raped, then I won't give them any more opportunities to rape me. No man will come close to me now, looking the way I do. The way I downplay my dressing. The clothes that I wear that are so unflattering to men that would repel them from putting me in a situation where we wouldn't be alone together.

At this stage in my life, I actually was the coordinator of the singles group at our church. I was in the praise and worship team and was learning more and drinking in every sermon that Perry was preaching on. Every word that God explained to him touched my soul and had great relevance to me. I remembered his words, a humble man who always told us that he gets his sermons from Jesus. He taught the congregation on how to walk in the way of God, his son Jesus, and that yes, the Holy Spirit is a HE, not an IT! That made me even closer to God and made me whole. That comment made the Holy Spirit, whom I didn't have much information about, useful.

Perry explained that happiness does not come in living with great wealth although there is nothing wrong with having it. That riches and wealth came from God, who intended to use it for the advancement of the Kingdom, His Kingdom, the power of His name, not our power wrapped up in it. The glory of the Kingdom could not be bought. Satan allows those who use cash improperly that way to expel themselves from the living God. Those who broker it for themselves to use for their glory, not His. Thy Kingdom come. Thy will be done. That is the responsibility of those who learn these principles and learn them early in their lives so that they can reap what they sow in the Kingdom of God. Satan is a liar and a great thief who follows those who don't heed the advice God gives to them in the scriptures. Scriptures that speak of the real power and the real Glory. His Glory, to come both now and forever more. Amen.

I received a call from my mother a week and a half later. She informed me that her pastor had confronted Glen with my accusations. After he lied again, the pastor and the board removed him from the church membership, and he was told never to return. *A pearl of great price*. I heard those words as I wrote this paragraph.

"Who, when he had found one **pearl of great price**, went and sold all that he had, and bought it. (Matthew 13:46)"

Jesus restored me. I was His "pearl of great price." He gave me great comfort. He healed my body, my mind, my deepest soul, and my spirit. He who hath healed me made me whole. Once again, I had become whole. Once more He made me whole. He made me. *me* again. The one whom he had chosen for this mission on earth. Who had adopted me to proclaim His love and affection, His divine goodness for all to see and come into Him. So that they too would be made whole again. At peace again. Able to love, and to seek His face in freedom here on earth as it is in Heaven. Divine healing made me whole.

And Jesus Christ still lives in my heart to this very day. He hath made me whole again. And righteous in His sight, which in turns has made me righteous in His knowledge that He loves me and comforts me for all that I have endured in this assignment on earth. In love and in devotion, I take this pledge to work for Him, and to fight for Him. No matter what comes my way. No matter what befalls me. He, Jesus, will fight my battles for me, just like He did King David against his enemies. He enriches my life for the Kingdom, and for HIS Glory. Forever more. Amen. For as long as I live, my life will be wrapped up in His Glory. Not my own, for the sake of His Kingdom and for the sake of His Glory. Forever and ever more. Amen

Isaiah 54 Common English Bible (CEB)

¹Sing, barren woman who has borne no child;
  break forth into singing and cry out,
   you who were never in labor,
  for the children of the wife who has been deserted will be more
numerous than the children of the married, says the LORD.
² Enlarge the site of your tent,
  and stretch out the drapes of your dwellings;
  don't hold back.
  Lengthen your tent ropes and strengthen your stakes.
³ To the right and to the left you will burst out,
  and your children will possess the nations' land
  and settle their desolate cities.

⁴ Don't fear,
  because you won't be ashamed;
  don't be dismayed,
  because you won't be disgraced.
You will forget the shame of your youth;
  you'll no longer remember the disgrace of your widowhood.
⁵ The one marrying you is the one who made you—
  the LORD of heavenly forces is his name.
The one redeeming you is the holy one of Israel,
  the one called the God of all the earth.
⁶ As an abandoned and dejected woman the LORD has summoned
you;
  as a young wife when she is rejected,
   says your God.
⁷ For a brief moment I abandoned you,
  but with great mercy I will bring you back.
⁸ In an outburst of rage,
  I hid my face from you for a moment,

but with everlasting love I have consoled you,
  says your redeemer, the LORD.

⁹ These are like the days of Noah for me,
  when I promised that Noah's waters would never again cover the
earth.
  Likewise I promise not to rage against you or rebuke you.
¹⁰ The mountains may shift,
  and the hills may be shaken,
  but my faithful love won't shift from you,
  and my covenant of peace won't be shaken,
  says the LORD, the one who pities you.

¹¹ Suffering one, storm-tossed, uncomforted,
  look, I am setting your gemstones in silvery metal
  and your foundations with sapphires.
¹² I will make your towers of rubies,
  and your gates of beryl,
  and all your walls of precious jewels.
¹³ All your children will be disciples of the LORD—
  I will make peace abound for your children.
¹⁴ You will be firmly founded in righteousness.
  You will stay far from oppression because you won't fear,
  far from terror because it won't come near you.
¹⁵ If anyone attacks you, it's none of my doing.
  Whoever attacks you will fall because of you.
¹⁶ Look, I myself created the metalworker who blows the fire of coal
and who produces a tool for his work.
  And I myself created the looter to destroy.
¹⁷ No weapon fashioned against you will succeed,
  and you may condemn every tongue that disputes with you.
This is the heritage of the LORD's servants,
  whose righteousness comes from me, says the LORD.

God is not predictable.

While at Grace, there were many whom I learned from who served in senior leadership. One couple in particular, Don and Nancy, pretty much set me on my path that would lead eventually to having courage to move on from my beloved church.

God changed my life to the degree to which I could feel it. My relationship to Him had never been this close. Now that I had been healed, I actually could have a personal relationship with my Jesus, not blocked or rocked by demeaning thoughts that, every day, bombarded me about my unworthiness to be in His presence. And I continued to grow from the teachings of Perry on Sundays. In fact, I looked forward to hearing him. After leaving work in Point Loma near the ocean, I would go straight to the church. I had many duties assigned to me by our pastor, which included the music ministry. As I grew in the knowledge of God, so did my contributions to the congregation.

I had become a partner with Pat Hood of a weekly home group of thirty-five or more on occasion as I said before. I had also become a lay counselor who helped counsel the flock. We had training, and were placed with those that needed to have longer sections than the leadership could provide. I enjoyed these ministries a lot. I enjoyed more the results of seeing people become more comfortable with themselves, or resolve issues with family members. But as He does, the Lord also wanted me to take on one more ministry.

Linda and David

I had been attending a singles group at Khilat Ariel that was led by my best friend, Linda. I loved their sessions and had made a number of endearing friendships. One day I asked Perry if we could begin a singles group for Grace. Perry did approve the idea. He was impressed by my growth in Jesus and had seen all the wonderful changes in my attitude and demeanor over the years. I had ceased being aloft and was now reaching out to others in making new friends. I no longer was afraid to start a conversation with people I'd never talked to before in the congregation, and even other places like grocery stores. I had the patience to listen to other people sharing their problems with me. My persona had changed dramatically from being unseen purposely to being an outgoing, happy inside and out woman.

And yes, I could now say the word woman without feeling shame for what had happened to me. That was a key comment, I no longer felt ashamed. I realized that a crime had occurred. Not because of anything I had done. The crime was done by a serial rapist who had plagued not only me, but other women. They may not have gotten a chance to regain their confidence because no one could teach the kind of themes I was receiving from Perry. Grace was my place of healing and receiving God's grace, and His personal touch both physically and mentally. Perry was not one to allow a new ministry into the church unless he saw you performing it. That gift would eventually be recognized if it bore good fruit. But he did allow me this ministry, as I had told him about the group I had been attending at Kehilat Ariel for so long.

The singles group started up a few months after Perry had given his permission. He announced it to the congregation, and more than a few turned up for the first meeting. The group grew from there to a rather large gathering numbering in the twenties. On a few occasions, our group and Linda Kerr, who led the Kehilat Ariel, would get together for movie nights or other fun single life events. This was fun, but more importantly it widened our lives as singles that weren't a part of our regular congregation. But little did I know that this would change in the future.

I played in the worship team at Grace with percussion instruments. I played the congas and the tambourine. I also had a microphone, asl was a backup vocal. One day Phil, the music director and Perry's brother, asked me to lead a song. The song had been a part of an ensemble of various professional Christian artists on a CD. The song was called "Be Bold and Be Strong" by the Maranatha Singers. I was scared to death. Unbeknownst to me, I had to venture out into a new realm of entertainment. One that suited me and my taste in music. I became more advanced in my skills as a singer and player in bands. Over the years I became more popular in performing in front of people my age and older. I perfected my skills as a musician and wrote a couple of songs that a band could sing in worship. I developed the talent to sing songs afterwards and became convinced that I could perform music in a band, with any band. A new setting for me, as I dragged my way out of my discomfort zone and into the hands of God, my Savior Jesus Christ.

Later in my life after at Kehilat Ariel, I began road trips with a band including Joann and Eric, my two best music partners who led it. They are now the primary music directors at Kehilat Ariel. Great there too. But I had learned a lot about myself and my fellow performers with Joanne and Erik. They allowed me to sing a little, but mainly I played instruments that I had purchased for my personal use. They belonged to me, so I could take them anywhere, which I did. A lot of times we would gather at different homes and drive to other events. We had a band of five under Joann and Erik at that time, and we traveled all over the place. Places where I would not have seen myself playing an instrument of any kind, much less singing vocals.

My interests improved to the point where I could take on any environment and believe that I could manage the situation. I sang songs of praise and worship. Words that praised God our Savior and our Heavenly Father. He gave me the courage to stand before people and to praise Him in all His Glory. I praised God with all my heart, soul, mind, and spirit. And afterwards, I would come off stage and lie down before God on my face and worship Him for the rest of the evening. I would cry for His presence. To be healed, and not to fail Him on stage when we sang together, just He and I. Just worshipping His holy and righteous name. Blessed be He Forever and ever. Amen! I had the very same experience when I would return from the teaching night with the singles.

I was blown away by the way God had manifested in the lesson I was teaching. I'd come home overwhelmed again with God's presence. I would lie on the floor and praise and worship Jesus for what He had said and done in the sessions. Again, very interesting. What God had me telling them was also the things I needed for myself. So, upon arriving home, I would reflect on what I had said as though I had been one of the ones sitting in the audience listening to me talk. Very surreal, but there you have it.

My life was fantastic at Grace. I had many friends who loved me, and I loved them just as much. I had been nurtured by our Pastor Perry with words straight from Heaven. He never let the singles go unnoticed in the congregation. If anything, he would think of ways to include them. He also encouraged them on being a part of the ministry there. Just because they hadn't married or had been divorced didn't make these issues disqualifying in God's eyes. He reminded them that Paul was single and had addressed that in the new covenant in the Gospel of Jesus. I Corinthians 7:7 -9 says,

> Sometimes I wish everyone were single like me—a simpler life in many ways! But celibacy is not for everyone any more than marriage is. God gives the gift of the single life to some, the gift of the married life to others.
>
> [8-9] I do, though, tell the unmarried and widows that singleness might well be the best thing for them, as it has been for me. But if they can't manage their desires and emotions, they should by all means go ahead and get married. The difficulties of marriage are preferable by far to a sexually tortured life as a single.

Perry encouraged singles to get involve in teaching children in Sunday school, joining the band like I had done, and going to prayer sessions that were being held in homes along with the home school methods presented by Jesus and His disciples who met in homes during and after Jesus's death. Perry called it the "inner circle." The outside ring was the job and friends; second ring was family, whether in marriage or single (with your parents or guardians). The third ring was church and the ministry. The last ring was your walk and what Jesus had called you to become. That was the most important of all because Jesus formed the catalyst as the most inner circle where everyone lived. We couldn't do any of the other rings well and completely unless we had the most holy of holies in the center. This lesson addressed all aspects of our lives as we lived it here on earth; on earth as it is in Heaven.

Jesus, being the center point, led the other rings to be done in God's ways, not ours or man's period. The single ring laid the foundation for the other rings to complete their journey toward wholeness in Jesus. As we Singles and other people in the congregation learned and moved forward in our walk with Jesus, we bloomed and blossomed into the children God had called us to be. So, you see how we in the congregation, whether single or married, rich or poor, overweight or...oh excuse me...whether young or old, could master our parts of what God had called us to do on earth without any excuse.

But my time in the ministry of Grace was coming to a close. And it really came quickly. And I was stunned by what God said to me, and yes. Afraid. I couldn't believe what I was hearing and didn't think I was hearing what I was hearing. I had to talk with Perry, and it had to be done quick.

The Lord told me to leave Grace.

God is obedience.

After decades there, in a loving, caring environment, seemingly under Heaven itself, my Lord and God Jesus Christ was asking me to leave Grace, my beloved Grace, and move my ministry to Kehilat Ariel. I had been attending Kehilat because of my friend Linda being there. I would attend Kehilat on a Saturday and Sunday.

When I first walked into Kehilat Ariel that first year, I began to cry. I don't know why. I didn't understand what to say or do. Most of the liturgy was in Hebrew. That included the songs. I wondered why, later, why I had cried so quickly. Now I know. It was when I first heard Hebrew words in a love song to me. The Hebrew language is such a perfect language. It is the language of God after all. I had often said in attempting to learn foreign languages that I should be able to since God tossed them out over a group of pagans. God knows them all! A few of my friends—Lyndia, Jeanette (Eme), and Ada—had the same experience upon their first visit. In fact, Lyndia said that she cried for two years, every time she entered the synagogue.

I finally regained my emotions and watched with great interest the other traditions. In the future, I came to know these traditions based in the Jewish culture and lifestyle. The Torah scrolls, the

Kaddish Cup, the Menorah, all would become very familiar to me in some intimate ways. The marching of the Torah scrolls among the audience was amazing! Look at that! What is that? What are they doing with it? What does this mean? The Torah scroll is ornate. A colorful wrapping covered the Torah itself. Like a mother would wrap a little tiny baby. There was a distinct Star of David on its front. I would learn later that the star is called a Mogen David. It represented King David's rule of the Hebrews during his reign in Jerusalem in 20 B.C. David ruled as a successful warrior and king over Israel forty years or more. He had been anointed king by Samuel the Prophet in 2 Samuel 2:7:

> So David went there, along with his two wives, Ahinoam from Jezreel and Abigail, Nabal's widow, from Carmel. [3] David also took the soldiers who were with him, each with his family, and they lived in the towns around Hebron. [4] Then the people of Judah came to Hebron and anointed David king over the house of Judah.
>
> When David was informed that it was the people of Jabesh-gilead who had buried Saul, [5] he sent messengers to the people of Jabesh-gilead. "The Lord bless you," he said to them, "for doing this loyal deed for your master Saul by burying him. [6] May the Lord now show you loyal love and faithfulness. I myself will also reward you because you did this. [7] So now take courage and be brave—yes, your master Saul is dead, but the house of

Judah has anointed me king over
them."

What was strange too about this Torah being marched among
the congregation was that this Torah had two sticks protruding out
of the middle of its "body." This represented the scroll that David
used to carry it among his own people. Especially when he danced
around it. He was glad to see in his day the carrying of this Torah
among his people in the city of David. He was amongst his people,
and he loved them all dearly. He spoke to the Lord about his love for
Him, and proclaimed this to him in verses in the bible. And in that
respect, telling us about his love for God and his caring of his
people. In case you wondered, God loves His chosen people and all
of us too. Also, He loves the children of God like David loved his own
children in his lifetime.

The two "sticks" protruding out of the body of the Torah
represent, as Rabbi Sholom Chein, said, "Trees of life; Atetz
Chayim."

"The 'atzei chayim' are the two wooden shafts attached to
either end of the Torah scrolls, around which it is rolled. Each shaft
is made long enough to extend beyond the top and bottom of the
scroll, and is used as a handle with which to hold the Sefer Torah
and to scroll from portion to portion."

I cried again when I was with the Torah. I didn't, again, know
why. But just accepted it. I wept into a tissue, covering my eyes at
times so others could not see my emotions. Didn't work. I just
assumed it would continue to happen, so I got comfortable with it.
No more embarrassment. The Lord was moving on me. For what
reason I didn't know. The Lord was taking me places I did not know.
His grace was sufficiency.

God is servant. Jeanette blessing the return of Sabbath for my Seder.

My tenure at KA was not brief. The Lord opened the door for me to experience and to explore. His countenance had found me a place I could call home. His countenance had placed me at a place where I could be free.

While at KA, my joy exploded. I learned to like the people there. We came together as family. I approached the rabbi to see if I could contribute to the congregation in any way. He told me that I could join the worship team whenever I became a member of the congregation. So, I tenured my request to join in the family I had now come to love. Once a member, I began to enjoy the atmosphere, and the relief I experienced was palatable. Since I had been on the worship team at Grace, I had gained much public experience with playing with a band and praising God on stage. I enjoyed this aspect of worship, as the experience of having the presence of God flow through you and your instruments was amazing. One may rehearse a song in practice, but how the Holy

Spirit allows it to come out as you are actually playing the song during worship is a different matter. Playing for the Lord is totally different than playing what you practiced. The practice to me was just that, rehearsal of a known song we already played, or perhaps learning a new one.

We waited until all had their parts down. All attention was on the song. But after the song had been perfected, and it'd played in front of an audience, there was a change. One example was when the KA worship band, named Yeshua's Remnant, played at the state fair every year. We would rehearse Jewish Messianic songs that were familiar to our congregation, but not necessarily familiar to the audience that attended the fair. To worship in the congregation that knew your music was wonderful, knowing most of the faces you see from the stage. It's easy to flow into the Spirit of God and have him hit your beats on the congas or other percussionist instruments. At the state fair, one may expect the atmosphere to be different, since you are essentially playing to a group of strangers. It isn't.

For me, in worship, the constant factor in the experience is being in the presence of God, feeling Him lead in whichever way that He wants you to play what was rehearsed. God may change the tempo to slow, or a pause in and of itself. In fact, if the entire band is worshiping in His presence, then everyone is touched by the Holy Spirit, and we still play the song in unison, but with maybe a different beginning in instruments. Or a slight hesitation whereby before, you came in on beat. The music is being enhanced by the Holy Spirit to touch the people you play in front of, no matter the people or the song. It is complicated to explain. But know that the Holy Spirit does come in to change what was perhaps rehearsed differently, but we are all in one and all together in the Messiah. The music is the same, just the Holy Spirit comes in and makes it more beautiful. And every band member picks up on His inspiration and connects it to the music we play.

At Grace, the experience of worship carried into the actual rehearsals. After learning a new song or rehearsing one we knew being prepared for the Sunday worship, we would actually feel the Holy Spirit as we played songs. We would close our eyes, play our instruments as the Holy Spirit led us, and sit silently afterward basking in His power and peace. Some songs in particular would bring in the spirit of the Ruch (Holy Spirit) so intensely; the band and the audience felt His presences. So strong! So believable! So WONDERFUL! Wow. What a blessing for all who were there. We had no livestreaming. And I truly believe that the Glory of God that we felt went out to those we loved, sitting in other regions or areas. We believed that there, at Grace. We were a force to be reckoned with. And the Ruch, who blessed us in our private rehearsals, blessed the congregation the next Sunday. The same at Kehilat Ariel. So joyful. So pleasing. So wonderful!

Kehilat Ariel's 2010 Seder and dancers

Prior to leaving Grace, I had put on a Passover Seder for the congregation opened to the public. I had asked Rabbi Barney to do the Seder and had asked the messianic dance team from KA to come too. Everything went well, and Grace was introduced to the Jewish culture of Yeshua the Messiah. Many were blessed and had never experienced the true Jesus the Christ as Yeshua Ha Messiah in Israel. This was important to me for many reasons. One of those reasons was that, having grown up in a Baptist church, I had never experienced the way God worked in the Middle East. We experienced our own version of the Holy Spirit, and its participation in our services was unique as usual, as in any service where his presence is welcomed. But it came to me, in my ministry to the of the living God, that much more was required. Much more knowledge of the way the Holy Spirit operated was needed in the main body of Christ, meaning His church of Jesus Christ the Messiah.

In his own way, Messiah had sacrificed a lot of his own humanity to teach us, in His humanity, how to live in Him: within Him, as we do today. He relinquished his sovereignty to do us a favor. A large favor. One of salvation in Him. In His Kingdom. Suffice it to say this favor was a huge one. One that embodied the giving and shedding of His blood to save us from our own sins. Sins, you remember, He did not partake of Himself while He lived on this earth. This planet. This planet that He and his Father created for our OWN GOOD! Not His own. For had he done it for his own glory on earth, nothing would have been accomplished. But since He, Jesus, died to Himself, He left the legacy for ALL of US to follow. His legacy of love, compassion, peace, peaceful coexistence in a world that didn't have that at the time. And is still struggling with that at this moment in OUR time.

So, here was a savior who had come to save the world from sin. Yet we eschewed him as a foreigner. A beggar in the ministry of "helps." A true deliverer was chastised by the rulers of His day as being an offshoot of a rebel whom they had to succumb in order not to stir up their "patrons." Now we see Jesus as He is now. A conqueror! A warrior! A battle-hardened solder! Hardened by the slings and literal arrows of the enemy Satan. Can His Kingdom be defeated? Can this magnificent Savior, who hung on the cross to bring us a blessing we could not perceive or hear of in His day, come as the savior of the world? Oh yes. Follow me, He said. Follow me to my Father. Because no one comes to my Father except through me. My flesh! My will! My life on this earth played the part in your being here at all, as I AM the creator of the universe and all it entails, says the Lord God Jesus.

So, let me be clear. Jesus, our Savior, is the only way, the only truth, that anyone on earth can come to the Almighty God, our Heavenly Father, in Heaven from earth. This earth is slowly passing away. But His truth, His legacy, Jesus's legacy, will NEVER PASS AWAY. He is the King of ALL Kings! And the Lord of ALL Lords. That includes the royal families in England, and around the world. Around the globe. Now remember this as you travel around. Because many will say that He, Jesus, had no power. Don't you believe them. He did. He does. And He still will when this earth no longer exists. I would ask you to accept Him as your personal, and I truly mean personal, Savior. Because He, Jesus, is the only way you will be saved from an eternal hell. A hell He and His father and the Holy Spirit created. Not for your soul, but for those demons who fell from grace out of Heaven. Be aware. Be alert. Do not be fooled by those who would take your soul and sell it to Satan. Because Satan is trying hard these days to take away, to snatch away, the victory you have in Jesus Christ. Don't let him. To that end, we will complete this book with this saying. As my earthly father said and we lived by in our home; "for me and my house, we will serve the Lord."

"And if it seem evil unto you to serve the Lord, choose you this day whom ye will serve, whether the gods which your fathers served

that were on the other side of the river, or the gods of the Amorites in whose land ye dwell. ***But as for me and my house, we will serve the Lord***. *(Joshua 24:15, 21st Century King James Version)"*

God's Destiny

I spoke earlier of a time when the Lord would speak to me about my destiny. He'd been very clear on it, and what was expected of me. I received specific details far into the future. Dreams would come to be, over a short time, more significant over longer periods. He talked with symbols. Lots of time during my prayer time with Him, I would receive visions that would again allow me to see what would happen. This to me took a lot of guesswork out of the question poised to people all the time at conventions or sermons. "Do you know what your destiny is?" I could always answer with an emphatic yes! However, WHEN this insight or revelation from God would happen was another question.

By this time in my service at Kehilat Ariel, my ministry involvement had increased substantially. I was asked to lead a women's group, which I did for a very short season. People would approach me at service or elsewhere to ask me to pray for or with them, which I was very pleased to accept and to do with much zeal. The interesting thing was that when I did pray for them, the prayer was always answered. This happened so often that I was frightened sometimes to ask God for things, in that I felt that I needed to be very careful as His answers for them and me came quickly.

I had also made it to the worship team as a percussionist. I taught myself how to play the congas, tambourine, and various Middle Eastern drums like the doumbek. I also learned other tempo instruments such as a cowbell, sticks, rain sticks, cymbals, chimes, and a host of other percussionist instruments. Our weekly worship team had evolved to become the main outreach team for the congregation. We had a drummer, pianist, flutist, clarinet, lead and bass guitars, and an especially prominent guitar that could play any style of music presented. The band members by that time were Mark as lead guitar along with Ken, Jeannie as pianist, Rene as flutist, Sue on clarinet, and her husband Mitch and Steve who switched off as drummers. Our Rabbi Barney Kasdan played the bass guitar and was the director of the music department. We formed the nucleus of the team called Yeshua's Remnant. Our team played for our congregation on Saturdays, but also made special appearances that spanned across the nation. We played conferences, churches, for Seders, at various malls with special presentations, and at the highest point of recognition outside our music genre, the San Diego County Fair.

We normally had a large stage to present our music, and that included the Messianic Dancers, who were a part of our team on many of these outreach occasions. We were paid for some of these outreaches to the public. Others were just gratuitous. Still others were to bless our Messianic community at various regional and international conferences where we played for free.

I had also become involved as the coordinator of the singles group, which I purposely made to ensure that the members received God's teaching and actually had a chance to date other singles of like-mindedness. These duties were similar to what I had done at Grace, and as Rabbi Barney said at the time, "Please select where you would like to serve." He was well aware of what I had been doing at Grace and felt comfortable saying that to me. God received all the glory, as after a lot of these outreaches and teachings ended, I would fall on my face before God and praise Him for how He had moved that night or day in the lives that He had asked me to serve for Him.

God is revealing.

Gradually the short interactions with He and I led to longer and longer encounters. I learned about God and how His word gave me new perceptions that I had never experienced. The Holy Spirit taught me just like He enlightened Paul and Peter and the other Apostles during their time after the Messiah had returned to Heaven. Let me just say here that Jesus never left "here." He is still HERE, on earth as He is in Heaven. This small but important difference is the key to the rest of this writing. The words "on earth as it is in Heaven" are crucial to understanding what I will relay to you in the coming chapters. And so, it continues.

When I started to journal, I was skeptical to say the very least. But later on, I could see the advantages in keeping a diary of what He said to me. Quite frankly, His words encompassed the upcoming events in my life. Of course, this got my attention. I was learning what would happen to me on a daily or monthly basis. And all turned out to be accurate.

You know, He, God, does speak kindly.

After I began to write in a journal, the content increased in volume and in direct communications with the Lord God. One of the learning techniques God gave me were books. Books He directed me to read. The content dealt with the intimacy between man and God himself. This reminded me later of the same intimacy that God

247

had with Adam and Eve. He encountered them on a daily basis. Not just when He wanted to instruct them or teach them something about their responsibilities, but also just to chat. Yes, Jesus actually does just chat. But his chat is much better than what you get from an online company.

Remember how God approached them after the encounter with the devil? He asked, "Where are you?" Now did He already know where they were? Yes. Did he also know what they had done? Yes. I believe God asked that question to see if the two of them would come over to Him and speak to Him face to face with the impact that had just been made by their disobedience. He wanted the two of them to tell Him what they had done was wrong, and how they were now suffering in their bodies and minds because of that. The mind because for the first time, something had come to block that communion of spirit between them and He.

What if their response had been, "Lord! Oh Lord. We have done something you told us not to do, and we are so heavy with feelings we have never experienced before. What is this sensation in our minds, our bodies, our spirit? We can hardly hear you speak now. Where are you our Lord God? Where are you?" Do you think that God would have had a different response than what actually happened? Because neither of them thought to do that.

The first thing that evil does is cloud your mind with doubt and fear. Fear of everything. Doubt about who you are and your future. Just one word like, *"We are lost and don't know how to get to you, Lord. Come find us and let us tell you what happened after we disobeyed what you told us not to do with that tree!"* Knowing the God of the scriptures and His character, perhaps his sentence that now stands today would not occur. He perhaps would have forgiven them for that disobedience and schooled them on how the evil one had fooled them.

Perhaps He would have said, "Let's fix your hearing and fears so that you and I can speak together again, just to ensure this doesn't happen again with that tree. You know, I was just testing you to see if you truly were faithful to me and what I think is good for you. That was all. Not to harm you. I love you both. I would never harm you." But that didn't happen. Adam, the first man, and Eve, the first woman, hid from God. They didn't answer when He called out to them in a beautiful place on earth called the "garden."

He places us in a garden, says David in the 23rd Psalm.

The Lord is my shepherd, I lack nothing;

He makes me lie down in green pastures,

he leads me beside quiet waters, ^{3} *he refreshes my soul.*

He guides me along the right paths

for his name's sake.

Jesus, He himself went to the Garden of Gethsemane to pray before the mob when Roman soldiers took Him away to be crucified. So instead of being in the Garden with God and happy, the two of them were hiding away from God.

"And they heard the sound of the Lord God walking in the garden in the cool of the day, and the man and his wife hid themselves from the presence of the Lord God among the trees of the garden. (Genesis 3:8)"

Now both Adam and Eve had become sad and eventually disillusioned because of their actions of not turning to God and repenting for their disobedience. You know, there wasn't anything like sin on earth between man and God until man became beholden to Satan. Then sin spread all over the earth, causing horrible things like murder and disease to spread among the people of earth. Murder and disease also were something new to the earth. So, the effect of sin hurt them and everyone to this day on earth. But there is hope still. Just like it would have been for Adam and Eve had they chosen to not go any further with evil, and repent. How? The verse 2 Peter 9 says, "The Lord is not slow about His promise, as some count slowness, but is patient toward you, *not wishing for any to perish but for all to come to repentance*. God would that no man would perish."

That desire of God and from God has never changed to this very day. God wants to save everyone on earth that He created. He has no desire to see His creation live in a horrible place called hell that was created for the father of evil/sin, the serpent Satan. Be that as it may, that is what is happening now due to sin. What if Adam and Eve had asked God to forgive them for their disobedience? Then we would have what we currently enjoy as Christians, as believers in Jesus the Messiah. We would possibly have an earth filled with God's love, on earth as it is in Heaven. We could have kept the eternity of immortality, the clear peace of mind. And the hope that our creator loved us enough to forgive anything we may have done. All without hesitation on His part or reservation.

What if? But we don't. And in a garden, much like the garden of disobedience of Adam and Eve's time, Jesus had to go to a garden to weep and pray for us. To give His life blood, soul, and spirit for us. To save us from the sin of disobedience made manifest on earth by Satan via Adam and Eve. Sad. Sad time, sad death. Painful death and beatings. Shame, hatred toward Him as He carried a cross, a tree trunk, to a barren outcrop of rocks. For us.

We'll never know why Adam and Eve didn't ask for forgiveness then. Who knows? But maybe, just maybe had they, perhaps we ourselves would not be suffering now as the result of their disobedience. And we and Jesus would be talking unhindered because of the grave and forgiveness of God. But that still can happen since Jesus did die for the sins of Adam and Eve. It's just going to take a while for His voice to sink into our souls and accept His offer.

Romans 8:26-28: *"In the same way the Spirit also helps our weakness; for we do not know how to pray as we should, but the Spirit Himself intercedes for us with groanings too deep for words; and He who searches the hearts knows what the mind of the Spirit is, because He intercedes for the saints according to the will of God.*

And we know that God causes all things to work together for good to those who love God, to those who are called according to His purpose. For those whom He foreknew, He also predestined to become conformed to the image of His Son, so that He would be the firstborn among many brethren; and these whom He predestined, He also called; and these whom He called, He also justified; and these whom He justified, He also glorified."

*And we know that God causes all things to work together for good to those who love God, to those who are called according to His purpose. *

The thoughts from God was the same in Adam and Eve's decades on earth. So, the answer: Jesus died for our sins including Adam and Eve's. And gave us the way out of the dilemma. And it has "worked together for good."

"Whereas are you? Where have you gone? Will you come to me, as I call you to be mine again?" All things happen to the glory of God.

And WHAT did they give up?

God is omnipresent, sovereign.

Genesis 5:21-24: "So all the days of Enoch amounted to 365 years. Enoch kept walking with the true God. Then he was no more, for God took him."

Or,

Jeremiah 29:11: "For I know the plans I have for you," declares the Lord, "plans to prosper you and not to harm you, plans to give you hope and a future."

Our **first couple** gave up total participation and communion and communication with God. Full communication. Total immersion in Him. Total involvement with the developing of a land created on earth by God to be enjoyed as if we were in the Heavenly realm itself WITH and TOTALLY connected in all senses. He created in us to enjoy Him and each other. Just think. Why would He create the sensation of joy and laughter on earth, as it is in Heaven? Why would He create a loving, caring, concerned (fruit of the spirit), peace if He Himself who holds within Himself would not want us to have it on earth?

Families like mine have exhibited these characteristics on earth during our lives as we grew up and as adults to this day. Perhaps a day will come when the earth will return to a type of Garden of Eden. God promised that too, talking about a "new Heaven" and a "new earth."

Revelation 21:1-5: "*I saw Heaven and earth new-created. Gone the first Heaven, gone the first earth, gone the sea.*

I saw Holy Jerusalem, new-created, descending resplendent out of Heaven, as ready for God as a bride for her husband.

I heard a voice thunder from the Throne: 'Look! Look! God has moved into the neighborhood, making his home with men and women! They're his people, he's their God. He'll wipe every tear from their eyes. Death is gone for good—tears gone, crying gone, pain gone—all the first order of things gone.' The Enthroned continued, 'Look! I'm making everything new. Write it all down— each word dependable and accurate.'"

God is omnipresent/righteous.

Angels

This was one of the most unusual parts of my journey with the Lord as I grew in His favor and knowledge. We can talk about how each of us are taught by the Holy Spirit. I do know that each of us has a destiny and a plan that is designed by God to ensure our ministry is completed here on earth. He does reward us as our desire to please the Trinity increases because of His love for us, and as we walk in His path.

Psalm 23:2-3: "*He makes me lie down in green pastures, he leads me beside quiet waters, he refreshes my soul. He guides me along the right paths for His name's sake.*"

I believe the word of God when the scriptures speak of Angels. They do exist. I want all that God has to offer, especially when it comes to what He wants me to have. We all have a destiny that correlates with our fellow believers in Messiah. Jesus will relay that destiny to you when you seek him earnestly, seek him first. Matthew 6:32-33: "*For after all these things do the Gentiles seek. For your heavenly Father knoweth that ye have need of all these things. But seek ye first the Kingdom of God and His righteousness, and all these things shall be added unto you.*"

That means having a desire to really get to know His desires for us on a personal basis. Have you had an occasion to come across someone in a chance meeting and suddenly feel joy or a special kinsmanship, a bond between you? That is similar to what is meant by a closeness that Jesus wants to establish with each of us from the very first, his new Christian disciple. Just like as a new believer, God has a destiny and a mission for you to complete on earth.

Jeremiah 29:13-14: "*For I know the plans I have for you,*" declares the Lord, "*plans to prosper you and not to harm you, plans to give you hope and a future. Then you will call on me and come and pray to me, and I will listen to you. You will seek me and find me when you seek me with all your heart."*

Likewise, angels have a mission. And whether you agree that they exist or not, God still assigns one to you. Permanently. And the angels are assigned to help you achieve that destiny of God's plans for you.

A. Genesis 19:1: The two **angels** arrived at Sodom in the evening, and Lot was sitting in the gateway of the city. When he saw them, he got up to meet them and bowed down with his face to the ground.

B. *Genesis 19:15: With the coming of dawn, the **angels** urged Lot, saying, "Hurry! Take your wife and your two daughters who are here, or you will be swept away when the city is punished."*

C. *Genesis 28:12: He had a dream in which he saw a stairway resting on the earth, with its top reaching to heaven, and the **angels** of God were ascending and descending on it.*

D. *Psalm 91:11: For he will command his **angels** concerning you to guard you in all your ways;*

E. *Psalm 103:20: Praise the Lord, you his **angels**, you mighty ones who do his bidding, who obey his word.*

F. *Matthew 4:11: Then the devil left him, and **angels** came and attended him.*

G. *Matthew 13:39: The harvest is the end of the age, and the harvesters are **angels**.*

H. *The **angel** said to the women, "Do not be afraid; for I know that you are looking for Jesus who has been crucified. He is not here, for He has risen, just as He said. Come, see the place where He was lying. Go quickly and tell His disciples that He has risen from the dead; and behold, He is going ahead of you into Galilee, there you will see Him; behold, I have told you."*

God has over time assigned more than a few angels to people on earth because of a need for teamwork to help accomplish goals in your life. We can use Lot as one example: *"With the coming of dawn, the **angels** urged Lot..."*

As my desire grew to know more about angels with whom I interacted, I sought books on this subject. I found many available in Christian bookstores and online. I began to gravitate toward authors on this subject including my mentors like Bobby Connors of Eagles View Ministry and Patricia King of Patricia King Ministry. I actually went to hear Mr. Connors speak at a conference in town. I'll never forget that. He signed a book that one of my friends had purchased for me one previous night. He put in a scripture verse for encouragement. In his book, Bobby teaches how to react if an angel visits with a message from God. He had, and still is, being visited by hundreds of angelic beings to convey various messages and assignments that had been given by the Lord God to inspire and help him complete his tasks. He wrote in his book *Heaven's Host: The Assignments of Angels—Both Faithful and Fallen,* "... ask their names" and "ask what the messages from Heaven were that they were to deliver."

Angels come to bring the word of God, messages, and other means for protection.

Psalms 91:11-12: *"For he will command his angels concerning you to guard you in all your ways; they will lift you up in their hands, so that you will not strike your foot against a stone."*

Imagine with me Mary's joy at marrying her soulmate Joseph, and having a child. But her sorrow at the circumstances too. But Mary's Uncle Zechariah made clear, between his duties and the Temple, the aspects of all that had happened for her. He himself had had a visit from an angel just before Elizabeth's pregnancy began. An archangel had spoken to him about his wife conceiving and having a child. A child that would be very special to the Kingdom of God.

Luke 1:30: *"But the angel said to her, "Do not be afraid, Mary; you have found favor with God."*

Zachariah had disbelieved his message from the archangel, and because of that doubt was made to become mute. In other words, he had been able to speak as anyone normally, and to speak the blessings in the inner sanctity of the Most High God. This is in fact where the archangel had spoken to him about his son to come. But he left the temple unable to speak, or even to provide an explanation for why he couldn't.

So, the crowd outside the temple, who were waiting for him to reappear after he had blessed their offerings, assumed that he actually had seen an angel. In other words, the crowd assumed that his being in such a place of pureness, standing before God and seeing him, that only an angel could have taken his voice away, but only as a SIGN from God to them. Now all they had to do was figure out why God had done this to him. But Zachariah knew.

Luke 1:19: *"Zechariah asked the angel, 'How can I be sure of this? I am an old man and my wife is well along in years.' The angel said to him, 'I am Gabriel. I stand in the presence of God, and I have been sent to speak to you and to tell you this good news. <u>And now you will be silent and not able to speak until the day this happens, because you did not believe my words, which will come true at their appointed time.</u>'"*

Their desire in that era in Jerusalem was to please God in any way they could, to make sure that all was well between them and Him. The crowd there questioned Zachariah from that day forward. But Zachariah could not respond, and resorted to using scrolls and instruments of writing in order to convey what he wanted or needed. Then, when his son John, now called John the Baptist, was born, Zachariah was given back his voice as the angel said he would. He could now speak after he named his son "John" instead of after his name. That was the norm.

Luke 1:59-66: *"On the eighth day they came to circumcise the child, and they were going to name him after his father Zechariah, <u>but his mother spoke up and said, 'No! He is to be called John.'</u>"*

"<u>They said to her, 'There is no one among your relatives who has that name.'</u>"

"Then they made signs to his father, to find out what he would like to name the child. <u>He asked for a writing tablet, and to everyone's astonishment he wrote, 'His name is John.' Immediately his mouth was opened and his tongue set free,</u> <u>and he began to speak, praising God</u>. All the neighbors were filled with awe, and throughout the hill country of Judea people were talking about all these things. Everyone who heard this wondered about it, asking, 'What then is this child going to be?' For the Lord's hand was with him."

This incident had happened almost a year prior to Mary's visit by the Angel Michael to announce her blessing of receiving a child from the Most High God.

Luke 1:34-38: *"'How will this be,' Mary asked the angel, 'since I am a virgin?'*

The angel answered, 'The Holy Spirit will come on you, and the power of the Most High will overshadow you. So, the holy one to be born will be called the Son of God. Even Elizabeth your relative is going to have a child in her old age, and she who was said to be unable to conceive is in her sixth month. For no word from God will ever fail.'"

And the importance of having a child that would be called the Messiah. The Savior of the Jewish nation. Yeshua ben David, Jesus son of David. Yeshua ben *Yadha'vov'ha*, Jesus son of God. And ALL these events in biblical history came about with a visit from an angel from the Most High God.

I never hear anyone talking about the blessing that each son got upon their birth or prior. In Mary's case she was at her cousin Elizabeth's home. So, I decided to add Mary's blessings here. Mary, mother of Jesus. Luke 1:46-56 said these blessings over her son Yeshua:

"And Mary said:

'My soul glorifies the Lord and my spirit rejoices in God my Savior, for he has been mindful of the humble state of his servant.

From now on all generations will call me blessed, for the Mighty One has done great things for me—holy is his name.

His mercy extends to those who fear him, from generation to generation.

He has performed mighty deeds with his arm; he has scattered those who are proud in their inmost thoughts.

He has brought down rulers from their thrones, but has lifted up the humble.

He has filled the hungry with good things but has sent the rich away empty.

He has helped his servant Israel, remembering to be merciful to Abraham and his descendants forever, just as he promised our ancestors.'"

What Zachariah said of John (The Baptist) was just as sweet.

Luke 1:67-79: *His father Zechariah was filled with the Holy Spirit and prophesied a song: 'Praise be to the Lord, the God of Israel, because he has come to his people and redeemed them. He has raised up a horn of salvation for us in the house of his servant David (as he said through his holy prophets of long ago), salvation from our enemies and from the hand of all who hate us—to show mercy to our ancestors and to remember his holy covenant, the oath he swore to our father Abraham: to rescue us from the hand of our enemies, and to enable us to serve him without fear in holiness and righteousness before him all our days.*

And you, my child, will be called a prophet of the Most High; for you will go on before the Lord to prepare the way for him, to give his people the knowledge of salvation through the forgiveness of their sins, because of the tender mercy of our God, by which the rising sun will come to us from heaven to shine on those living in darkness and in the shadow of death, to guide our feet into the path of peace.'"

Now you've seen how scriptures tell us that angels are around us, that continues even now. We all have been assigned angles.

Hebrew 1:14: *"Are not all angels ministering spirits sent to serve those who will inherit salvation?"*

The one permanent angel assigned to us will take us to Heaven when it's time to pass over into that realm of peace. I want all that God has to offer, especially when it comes to what He wants me to have. I do know the names of my angels, and yes, I have a few that were told to me that would work with me for certain reasons. My permanent angel's name is **Weapon**. And the verse given to me by the Lord God was one of my favorites.

Isaiah 54:17 says: *"'No weapon formed against you shall prosper, And every tongue which rises against you in judgment You shall condemn. This is the heritage of the servants of the Lord, And their righteousness is from Me,' Says the Lord."*

I asked the Lord to see his appearance, and the Lord God did. He is a very tall angel, with a large wingspan. Huge wings! The angel stood there in front of me, smiling. His garb was like a Roman solder's outfit. He was a warrior. His upper body had a type of armor that was real. Not fake like in the movies that show the Roman soldiers' muscles. He was elevated in the air above my bed. His color seemingly looked like milk chocolate. Creamy. His hair was black. His arms were by his side. That smile just fixated me. He was so happy! He was such a warrior! And I asked God about him, the scripture God gave about "no weapon formed against you will prosper." So, I call him Weapon! He has been in many dreams of importance to my life. All those dreams were from God. He used Weapon to convey His message of our mother's death in a dream.

I also have one called the Angel of Supply. I saw him one night while going to sleep. He came to me, and he wore light grayish clothing, which looked like staked robes. But were properly fitted and looked regal. I asked him what his name was, and what was his message. He said, "I am here to go before you..." To my chagrin, I fell asleep. I was so tired I couldn't stay awake. I felt I had embarrassed myself, and was angry at myself for falling off. I know the angel still spoke to my holy spirit living inside me. His message was to assure that I had ALL the financial needs covered in the future. How reassuring from God!

The other angels' names are Strong Man, who is out in the galaxy, and two male twin angels dressed in various garb when sending me messages in dreams. Also, there are four women Chinese angels who come in dreams to tell me an event will happen. That included the upcoming deaths of some people I knew, and future traumatic incidents that will come to our nation.

Then there are two male guards, one black, one white. One is younger with a backpack and dressed in jeans like a college student going to classes. The older angel has on a guard uniform. There are two male angels called Twins. They come to announce future things to me, mainly in dreams. They told me about my boss, who was going to be in trouble soon. He was fired as it played out later. They wear various uniforms depending on the message that was given. One was about me retiring. There are two separate male angels from England. One is dressed in an 18th century British uniform as an officer. He had a message for me about England, which I took down in my journal after the visit in a vision. Prior to his giving me the message and after I asked him his name (his name is Sentinel), he showed me his red dress uniform, which had an incredible pure white cuff with material that dazzled! And the other English angel I call centurion. He is dressed as a Roman soldier with his uniform with a red velvet tunic and armor, complete with a helmet with a plume of a senior commander. He guards me, and God sends me dreams and visions of him doing things in the name of God. Lately, God has assigned a new angel whose name is Destiny. Why am I not surprised?

Jeremiah 29:11-13 New International Version (NIV): "'For I know the plans I have for you,' declares the Lord, 'plans to prosper you and not to harm you, plans to give you hope and a future. Then you will call on me and come and pray to me, and I will listen to you. You will seek me and find me when you seek me with all your heart.'"

Well that is the pack, my herd of angels in my life. They have come to me in dreams and visions carrying messages of sadness, of national importance, and warnings of upcoming personal events in my life. As Bobby Conner's said, ask them their names and their mission for God. And as the scripture says in Psalm 91:11, *"For He shall give His angels charge over you, to keep you in all your ways."*

God is timeless

Timing is an issue, a very important issue.

What do you think of Almighty God taking King Saul to task for offering a sacrifice after Samuel the Prophet asked him to wait until he had arrived? Do you remember when God asked David not to count the number of the Israelites in camp? What about when Joseph, the earthly father of Jesus, was told to leave where he and the baby were staying and quickly move to Egypt? Joseph and Miriam stayed there until Herod the Great died, then returned to their homeland. What if Joseph had mistimed that move back? And by the way, WHO is telling these men and women what to do, when to do it, and where to go?

In this present time in our country, there is division, lack of unity among people and ethnic groups, and lawlessness by terrorists all over, such as horrific murders of people using crucifixion. Bodies drawn and quartered, stabbed and dismembered with machetes. Political strife, and deceitful practices amongst government institutions toward elected members of the society. And not to forget that the ones responsible for running nations and countries, whether dictatorships or socialism, have begun the slow march into mayhem with lack of honesty and clarity toward the people living in their land. And this was going on in Herod's day. I wonder what will happen to our nation if we start down the same distressful path. Oh! We ARE there, now!

Throughout the history of mankind on this earth, God Almighty, Yeshua the Messiah, and the Holy Spirit have had to operate under the same type of sin that plagued the early existence of our world. This was not created to be this way. But sin does that to a people, a nation, a country, a state, territory among the world. Sin pollutes the atmosphere. And such is the case in our current circumstances in our nation.

God Almighty's timing sent Samuel to save the nation of Israel from the misguided leadership of King Saul.

*1 Samuel 13:13-14: "'That was a fool thing to do,' Samuel said to **Saul**. "If you had kept the appointment that your God commanded, by now God would have set a firm and lasting foundation under your **kingly** rule over Israel. As it is, your **kingly** rule is already falling to pieces. God is out looking for your replacement right now. This time he'll do the choosing. When he finds him, he'll appoint him leader of his people. <u>And all because you didn't keep your appointment with God!</u>'"*

You can see His timing as to when the Son of Man came to the earth. King David's rulership had set Israel up in Jerusalem to be the greatest nation of its time. And even the ascension to being King of Israel came decades after Samuel anointed him to be so. Every nation on earth came to see him and his sons. Solomon taught them how to govern their own countries. God's timing placed Jesus in such a period of time mainly because Isaiah, Ezekiel, Amos, Hosea, Jeremiah, and the other major prophets told God's chosen people of how He would deliver them from their oppressors and enemies.

Many more examples of God's timing concerning issues in our world can be found in the Book of Ester, where Ester had to stand up for the Jews in Babylon (Esther 7:1-9; 8:1-16). Urged on by her uncle Mordechai, she revealed her heritage to her husband one night as he sat holding court on his throne. She was successful. In the Book of Ruth, Ruth's mother-in-law retreated or returned to her mother country as her husband and all her sons had died. Ruth, one of her daughters-in-law, decided not to stay in Moab, and to leave with her mother-in-law Naomi. Both returned to Israel, Naomi's homeland (Ruth, Chapter 2). While there, Naomi sent Ruth to "glean" for grain at her relative Boaz's private fields (Ruth 2:3), which were lush and plentiful. Ruth would bundle her apron as a cloth to fill with heaps of grain left on purpose to take back to Naomi for their food.

Imagine if Ruth had not been so industrious one day, and left off going to the grounds. Timing. She would have missed an opportunity set up by God that would bring about a drastic change in all their living circumstances. Timing the day of the Lord, that day for Ruth allowed Boaz, Naomi's relative, to see her picking up the scraps of grain left over by the field workers. That day, that very day and days after, Ruth found more grain to pick up than at any other time previously doing this chore. She didn't know that this was due to Boaz's order to the field workers to leave LOTS behind them of grain for this beautiful woman he had seen at the edge of the field picking up the leftovers that had fallen.

When Ruth told Naomi, what had happened that day, Naomi told her to prepare herself for a visit to Boaz's fields. One evening, Naomi told Ruth to go to his barn, and lay at the feet of his place of rest. As Boaz awoken to something in the room, he saw the same beautiful woman who had been picking up the grains in his fields. He sent her home to Naomi. This ritual of laying at the feet of man was not unusual at that time. It meant submission and trust by the person doing it toward the person to whom it was being done. After Ruth returned before dawn, Naomi knew that her daughter-in-law had just submitted herself to her new husband. In fact, she told Ruth this. "'Go to bed and sleep. The man will not let this matter rest until he has done what he intends to do toward you.' 'Sit tight, my daughter,' Naomi replied, 'until you know how it turns out. The man won't rest until he resolves the matter today.'

And Boaz didn't let "the matter rest." He contacted his own relatives to clear the path to ask Ruth to marry him. She and Boaz became parents to a boy, who you can read about in the scriptures as being in the direct line of the family tree from whence came the Messiah. Jesus the Messiah. Timing? Yes. But I also believe that God would have allowed this union to come about, if not on that day, but one close. Why? Because in matters of the Kingdom, God's hand moves to ensure that "matters" and "issues" have their time in His perfect timing.

Isn't it wonderful that although we want to make sure we are doing what He asks us to do at the time, that if we slip up, he is there to rectify the issue? Or reboot to make it all good. I have sometimes berated myself for not taking the appropriate steps to ensure my own living environment. I think I have moved in San Diego and around San Diego County so much that I may have covered the entire region. Now, not to say all the moves were bad, but I did not consult the Lord about his opinion during that time. Or I did, but didn't want to hear what His answer was. So, I moved ahead.

I have spoken of timing. Every time I moved and had to move again, God supplied my escape. Be it having to sell my home on a slow market, or being told to move so the home I was living in could be sold. Or at work where I short-sighted myself and turned down two jobs that would have made me a manager. Had I accepted those positions, I believe that I would have not gone through some of the very unpleasant situations where I worked. And finances would not have been an issue. But timing is important, and as I wish now that I could have avoided some pain in my life, God always blessed me. Not because of the consequences of what those decisions were, but because no matter how I messed up, He controlled all things in time.

Let me explain. I did things that God told me not to do. In that regard, my mistakes, not serious, caused me to miss many opportunities that God had specifically told me would happen. Some were not taking an opportunity to play in a large church band. Similarly, not taking an opportunity to teach my congas to another large church's music team. Another was not following God's voice on some crucial actions that would have brought in a large sum of money, using my music talent again. That cost me a new home, and a better situation than where I am now.

When God told me these things in a two- to almost five-day conference, I was devastated. I wondered why certain things weren't panning out as Jesus and other prophets had said to me. I now know that those things will be impossible to have, as I missed the timing of the events. My fault. Not God's. My lack of courage to take on these and other opportunities out of fear, and loathing of my body, which kept God from giving me that blessing He had for me. And the others who would have been blessed had I done what God asked me to do in those "moments of time." Lost out. As did others perhaps. But I believe that God made a way for them to carry on, in spite of my lack of confidence in myself.

Yes, God can redeem the time. And there are ample scriptures in the Bible that tell us of that. But in my case, I learned the hard way that you have to measure up to what God is asking you to do. And don't take it lightly. Timing is crucial. Can't always return to it, or have a do-over. As that "still very small voice" is not kidding when He asks us to take on other responsivities that may, at that time, seem out of the ordinary. Out of your comfort zone. Out of your belief or faith that you can do. Such was and is my lot. I carry this disappointment with me. Mainly because I feel I've let God down in His plan for my life in those years I squandered doing other things or nothing. Nothing like fear to keep you from going further in the Kingdom of God. So, let me be frank. It was not God's fault that I messed up those great opportunities. My omissions were my fault, for which I asked God to forgive me. His role is to take us up and on to our work for the Kingdom. If, and only if, we do that when He asks us to, and not hesitate like I did, no doubt we will land on our promises made to us via His word. Timing.

Now I didn't realize how seriously my action caused me to lose out. And like the Israelites, not taking the advice of Joshua and Kaleb to take the land, their consequences cost them greatly. Mine has too. I may have missed some opportunities in my past due to my poor actions. But I assure you. I will not miss those future opportunities that God had ready from the time I was conceived in my mother's womb, that are now before me. This book is an example of my poor timing. The Lord God told me that this timing is late. But here it is. After all the missing of other good things that would have made my life different, this one got out. God does redeem the time. But just like Israelites, some things can't be redone. I face that now with gratitude and respect for God and His ways. But as God says in Romans 8:27-28:

"And he who searches our hearts knows the mind of the Spirit, because the Spirit intercedes for God's people in accordance with the will of God. <u>And we know that in all things God works for the good of those who love him, who have been called according to his purpose."</u>

Yes, there are consequences. But also, yes, the best is yet to come for me as well.

Being in control, and after I repented to him with sincerity, He designed it so I could still reach the goals He set for me. And yet I met people whom I would not have known where I made the wrong decision. That took the sting out of it for me after reflections. I just wonder how the ones I didn't meet would have been like. Timing yes, but the Father of time and eternity holds that in His hand. As He does us. Reboot.

God is honoring.

Yes, He does tell us private issues that may or may not be obtained any other way. And He may tell us to do things we might ordinarily not do. It's our job to open up to Him and obey and behave properly. As we understand Him more, we become better for it. It's our job to be there. Not to be lazy and not comply. He is the one who has the power of the pen, the power of the thought. He may have those He wants to consider for other positions in Glory. Or He may not consider those He considered before on earth. Samson, a physically strong and capable leader for Israel, mirrors mankind's will or desire to follow through with their destinies on earth. I myself have taken to placing the blame on the Lord that He clearly had nothing to do with in my own failures. More than once, I've misapplied or lacked the discernment to fully wait for the word to become clearer. I disappointed the Lord and made it hard for Him to help me. There is a part of me that always thinks that when I didn't get it right, He'll forgive and allow me to continue. And He did. He does.

Honor. Honor is looked upon by the Lord as a promise. One verse speaks to that. Ephesians 6:2 says, "Honor thy father and mother," which is the first commandment with promise..." The Promise? Verse 3: "that it may be well with thee, and thou mayest live long on the earth." Yeshua certainly honored His Father with his actions and his obedience to follow His Father's path and life as a pattern. This verse was recited a lot in our family as I grew up. Sometimes for correction, other times to be reminded to be respectful toward our mom or dad. More so to us as adults, as we were met with peer pressure to slip away and ditch school, or to disobey something or a principle that our parents taught us. Mostly the latter. When we did comply, it indicated to our parents that we could be trusted to go elsewhere with others.

Thy shall not steal, thy shall not bear witness falsely against others. Collectively, these verses form the idea that we take into consideration how we affect others by our own actions whether good or bad. In Mama and Daddy's case, in order for us to honor them and our good family name, it was to act as if they were standing beside us as we made the decision. And isn't that what God does? He is invisible, but He really is standing right beside us every minute, every second of the day. We carry Him in our hearts, which goes everywhere we go. We transport him to destinations that either he would be thrilled to be seen at, or to places it wouldn't be good for his righteousness sake to have Him there. The apostles witnessed this on a daily basis as Yeshua led them on their destinies to become his teachers on earth after His departure. Likewise, the Father hears us when we speak or even when we **think** thoughts. He does know our mind. We don't always have to be speak audibly for Him to hear us speak or think. That is why Moshe spoke:

*"The Lord **talked** with you face to face in the mount out of the midst of the fire" (Deuteronomy 5:4).*

*"And ye said, 'Behold, the Lord our God hath shown us His glory and His greatness, and we have heard His voice out of the midst of the fire. We have seen this day that God doth **talk** with man, and he liveth"* (Deuteronomy 5:24).

Exodus 33:9: And it came to pass, as Moses entered into the tabernacle, the pillar of cloud descended and stood at the door of the tabernacle, and the Lord **talked** with Moses.

When the Lord speaks to you, He also desires a conversation with you. You can even initiate a conversation with Him. King David asked in 1 Samuel whether he should go up and attack their enemies.

"And David inquired of the Lord, saying, Shall I pursue this troop? Shall I overtake them? **The Lord answered him, Pursue, for you shall surely overtake them and without fail recover all**" (1 Samuel 30:8).

"David **recovered all that** the Amalekites had taken and rescued his two wives" (1 Samuel 30:18).

"Nothing was missing, small or great, sons or daughters, spoil or anything that had been taken; David recovered all" (1 Samuel 30:19).

Intimacy between King David and God Almighty had developed over the trying years, as David had to survive under threats of death from King Saul and Israel's many enemies. Some may ask why I keep saying that interaction is needed when we come into the Kingdom of the Most High Almighty God our Father, Yeshua the Messiah, and the Ruch Ha Kadesh. We were meant to have that personal intimacy with God whom He created. It's a good start for those who want to, and an encouragement to those who already are on that road to even deeper times of intimacy with the Lord. Honor His presence.

Be His army for the destiny He has, or will, spell out for you. If only you would ask.

I will end this book with this. I am in the family of God, my kinsman redeemers. For His sake, I follow more closely His ways, as I did my earthly Father and Mother. And it's for His sake, God's sake, that I do the work in His Kingdom that he assigns me to do. The Kingdom of God is forever. Israel is forever. Just like King David and others, I too have a role to play in this Kingdom of actors. This Kingdom of Glory. His Kingdom on earth, where the Ancient of Days, (Yeshua) Jesus, and the Holy Spirit (Ruch), planted the seed and saw it grow. To God be the Glory forever and ever and ever. Amen!

Dor l' Dor. Shalom.

THE TAYLORSVILLE TIMES, WEDNESDAY, OCTOBER 6, 2010   15A

November 7 is date for area Alzheimer's Memory Walk

Lucille Mayes Honored at 92nd birthday celebration Saturday

Family and friends of Mrs. Harve (Lucille) Mayes of Taylorsville gathered at noon on Saturday, October 2, 2010 at Macedonia Baptist Church to celebrate her 92nd birthday. Her seven children along with four individuals who were afforded a home in the Mayes' home hold are shown with the birthday lady. Shown from the left seated are: James Mayes, Howard Mayes, Jessie Mayes, Mrs. Harve (Lucille) Mayes, Betty M. Lackey, Mary Annabelleth Mayes, standing: Harve Junior Mayes, Sterling Pittman, Mildred Williams, Wilma Hazell, Bonnie Gene Howell, and Bonnie Mayes.

Alexander Baptist Association 123rd Annual Session is Oct. 14

Sain receives BCDA's Clayton Teague Award September 25

GARY SAIN

Residents urged to participate in Clean Alexander Day Oct. 30

Karate tourney at ACHS Sat., October 9

Homecoming set Oct. 24 at Shiloh Lutheran

HHS Class of '69 plans reunion

Pink Ribbon Day at Carmen's Greenhouse

Hiddenite High School Class of '63 plans reunion

Alexander Central Class of 2000 plans reunion October 15

Coming Live To The
Alexander Central Auditorium

THE INSPIRATIONS

Opening Group - Jordan Dagenhart & Family

Saturday, October 9, 2010 • 7:00 PM

Alexander Central Auditorium

Advanced Tickets $15 • At The Door $20

Bibliography of Mammy Judy

ACLU Briefing Paper. Racial Justice.
www.aclu.org/library/pbp11.html

Britannica Online. Black code. Britannica Encyclopedia, 1997.
www.britannica.com/topic/black-code

Douglass, Frederick. *Narrative of the Life of Frederick Douglass, an American Slave, Written by Himself*. The Norton Anthology of African American Literature, 1997.

Excerpts from U.S. Slave Law. Handout.

Grinton, Elizabeth E. B. *Treasure Troves*. Unpublished manuscript.

The Norton Anthology of African American Literature. W. W. Norton Company, 1997.

Slave Information from Various Loudoun Co., VA documents.
www.rootsweb.com/~inclinto/slaves.html

CPSIA information can be obtained
at www.ICGtesting.com
Printed in the USA
LVHW050457171120
671903LV00003B/125